DEDICATION

HAL

To the writers, may your words improve the world in ways you have yet to even imagine.

STEVE

This book is dedicated to the five most important people in my life whom I love more than words can say.

To mom, thanks for always being there and for showing me what it means to selflessly take care of the people you love.

To the "Three Genes." My father who constantly gives great advice (even if it's in a PowerPoint presentation), my brother who protected me (even when I deserved a butt whooping), and my son who changed my world as soon as he entered it.

To my amazing wife Kristin, who patiently listens to my crazy ideas without judging me. I'll always be your big stinker!

CONTENTS

FOREWORD BY JAMES ALTUCHER

The MIRACLE MORNING for WRITERS

How to Build a Writing Ritual That Increases Your Impact and Your Income

Hal Elrod & Steve Scott

With Honorée Corder

THE MIRACLE MORNING FOR WRITERS

Hal Elrod & Steve Scott
with Honorée Corder

Interior Design: Christina Culbertson, 3CsBooks.com

A SPECIAL INVITATION FROM HAL

Fans and readers of *The Miracle Morning* make up an extraordinary community of like-minded individuals who wake up each day dedicated to fulfilling the unlimited potential that is within all of us. As the author of *The Miracle Morning*, it was my desire to create an online space where readers and fans could go to connect, get encouragement, share best practices, support one another, discuss the book, post videos, find an accountability partner, and even swap smoothie recipes and exercise routines.

I honestly had no idea that The Miracle Morning Community would become one of the most inspiring, engaged, and supportive online communities in the world, but it has. I'm blown away by the caliber of our 40,000+ members, which consists of people from all around the globe and is growing daily.

Just go to **www.MyTMMCommunity.com** and request to join The Miracle Morning Community (on Facebook). Here you'll be able to connect with others who are already practicing The Miracle Morning—many of whom have been doing it for years—to get additional support and accelerate your success.

I'll be moderating the community and checking in regularly. I look forward to seeing you there!

If you'd like to connect with me personally on social media, follow **@HalElrod** on Twitter and **Facebook.com/YoPalHal** on Facebook. Please feel free to send me a direct message, leave a comment, or ask me a question. I do my best to answer every single one, so let's connect soon!

FOREWORD
BY JAMES ALTUCHER

I can't believe three of my favorite authors asked me to write a Foreword to their book, *The Miracle Morning for Writers*.

I feel like the new drummer of the Rolling Stones.

Writing is hard. You have to sit for hours and type letters. You have to think of things that nobody ever thought of and tell them in ways that nobody ever told them before.

Humans weren't made to sit and write for hours. We were made to hunt and gather. And climb trees. Or whatever they did back then.

People say, "Every idea has been done."

This is not true. The world lives in a giant comfort zone. A good writer's job is to take us outside that comfort zone, to see something new inside of something old.

When I write, I'm terrified. I want to be able to say something new. I want to say it in an entertaining way. I want to be scared to hit publish. (If I'm not scared to write it, nobody will be scared—or even shocked—to read it.) I want to take chances (else, how will I grow?). I want readers to say, "I can't believe he just said that!"

When I wrote the book *Choose Yourself!* I started off talking about how, at my worst moments, I wished I were dead.

Then I wrote about how I came back from that wish. How I thrived after having such a horrible wish. How my wishes didn't come true.

The goal of the book was not to give advice. But advice is autobiography. The best any writer can do is tell a good story—not preach from a pedestal or give advice with no backbone.

This is a book that seems to be about writing. But not really. Again ... advice is autobiography. This is a book by writers, and the story is how they do this amazingly difficult thing that humans were never meant to do.

Hal Elrod has written *The Miracle Morning,* which is not only a massive bestseller, but also the story of how he literally came back from death.

It's not about how you can come back from death. It's Hal's story. But it's a big enough story that it has literally inspired millions to try out and follow a path similar to Hal's. To establish their own healthy morning routines so they can come back from whatever deaths are in their lives.

I love how Honorée Corder then took this simple idea and made it accessible for many other categories in her own writing. She took *The Miracle Morning* and then wrote X, Y, and Z.

And now this book.

I follow a Miracle Morning routine as well, and I am grateful for it.

Steve Scott has written dozens of books. I can't even keep track of the number of books Steve (and his alter ego, SJ) have written.

When I first started seeing Steve's name all over the bestseller lists I knew I had to call him and ask him how he did it. So I did, and he told me.

Now he's telling you in this book. He's not telling you what to do. He's telling you how he did it. And how he makes a great living doing it.

I follow a morning routine for my writing. If I didn't, I would never write. I've written 18 books. I have a children's book coming out soon. I have a book on mentorship coming out soon.

And I hope to write many other books in my life.

Writing is an IV transfusion directly into my soul. It takes out the bad blood inside me and puts in good blood. Without a Daily Writing Routine, I think I still would be dead, or stuck, or unhappy, or unsatisfied, and I would have less opportunity and fewer friends in my life.

Hal, Steve, and Honorée are my friends—entirely because I write and that's how we met and bonded.

I wake up, I exercise, I shower, I read, I drink coffee, I play around with ideas, and then the writing begins.

I can go into more detail of this routine. Particularly what I read to inspire my writing. And how I come up with ideas. And how I mine my past to dig for gems that I haven't discovered before. And how I put words together to tell a story that I think will be fun for people to read.

But that would take an entire book.

And instead, Honorée, Hal, and Steve have written *the* book. I know that what they describe works. Because it works for them, and I have seen a routine work for me.

I know it will work for you also.

James Altucher, Entrepreneur and Best-Selling Author

www.jamesaltucher.com

INTRODUCTION
BY STEVE SCOTT

I have a secret weapon for my writing routine…

Each morning, I wake up, complete a series of habits, and fire up my laptop ready to share my thoughts with the world. I don't feel sleepy or groggy like most people do during those early hours. Instead, my mind is clear, and I enjoy a heightened sense of motivation to write. The reason why? It's because of the Miracle Morning.

As a writer, it's important to manage your energy level. The craft we've chosen is amazing, but it's also one of the most sedentary ways to spend your time. So what the Miracle Morning gives you is a chance to start the day on the right foot with the opportunity to improve your mind and body.

In *The 7 Habits of Highly Effective People*, Stephen Covey writes about the importance of prioritizing the activities that are important but not urgent. He defines important activities as the things that are critical to accomplishing your long-term goals, but have no inherent deadline; they are easy to put off in lieu of more urgent, and less important, tasks.

We all know it's important to exercise, read, and eat healthy foods because these habits will have a significant long-term impact on your life, but they are often put on the back burner when something urgent comes up. Like when an important work project gets thrown in your lap.

What the Miracle Morning gives you is a special time of the day when you complete those important but not urgent activities. By combining silence, visualization, journaling, reading, affirmations, and exercise, you have an opportunity to complete those crucial activities before most people even get out of bed. Activities that will have a cumulative, positive long-term impact on your writing success.

As you'll see below, I'm a fairly recent convert to the Life S.A.V.E.R.S. method created by Hal. Since adopting these habits, my writing (and motivation for this habit) has reached new heights. Now I'd consider it to be one of the important parts of my day.

From Night Owl to Early Bird

My story starts with a lot of frustration. In early 2012, I was obsessed with this crazy idea of becoming a successful self-published author. The problem? I wasn't a very consistent writer.

I approached my writing with a feast or famine attitude. Some days, I would crank out a few thousand words, but then these were followed by days where I didn't write a single word. This situation was frustrating because, while I wanted to build this habit, I couldn't figure out how to make it consistent.

Eventually, I made a decision that forever changed my life. Instead of finding time to write, I made the commitment to get up in the morning and complete my words before doing anything else. My logic was simple—if I wrote first thing in the morning, then this would eliminate any excuses for not completing my daily words.

Unfortunately there was one, small hiccup in this plan ...

I hated getting up in the morning.

You see, I have lived the laptop lifestyle since 2004, so I believed that I could get up whenever I wanted. I was a night owl who enjoyed working late into the evening, so it was okay to sleep until 11:00 a.m. and then start my day.

But what I quickly found is that this lifestyle was hindering my writing. By the time I got up, ate lunch, and started my day, the last thing I wanted to do was write.

Eventually, I came to see the light. While I enjoy sleeping in as much as the next guy (or gal), I made the commitment to set my alarm clock for the unimaginable time of 9:00 a.m. and then immediately start writing.

At first this new routine was a major struggle. There were many mornings when I'd hit the snooze button and immediately go back to sleep. But eventually I consistently forced myself out of bed and started my writing day.

Unfortunately, during this time I soon realized that getting up early wasn't enough. While I was physically present, my mind was foggy, and I felt very uncreative. I made another decision that would change my life: I started each day with a morning routine.

At first, my morning ritual included habits that I read about when I did a Google search. I wrote down my goals, exercised for a bit, identified the important tasks for the day, and read quality books. While these activities helped my writing, I felt there was something missing.

A year later, I heard about *The Miracle Morning* by Hal Elrod. It seemed like everyone was talking about this book and how it had changed their lives. And when I finally got around to reading it, I discovered why people loved it.

What Hal teaches is a proven routine that focuses on the six habits that have had the biggest impact on the lives of successful people. He doesn't just tell you to complete a morning routine he shows you exactly what to do and when to do it.

Since implementing the Miracle Morning practice, my writing (and personal) success has vastly improved. I now start each session motivated and ready to crank out a few thousand words.

Even better, my mind is crystal clear, and I never experience any type of writer's block.

The Miracle Morning has also had significant impact on my business. I've written over a dozen bestselling titles, generated a multiple six-figure yearly income, and even had a book land on *The Wall Street Journal* Best Selling Books list. All of this success is due to that one decision to get up early in the morning, complete a series of positive habits, and then start writing before doing anything else.

The Miracle Morning for Writers

As you'll learn, the most successful writers complete their words first thing in the morning. Sure, some work late in the evening or when they can find the time. But if you study the habits of professional authors, you'll see that most of them get up early and complete their words before the afternoon.

It's actually not that hard to write thousands of words on a daily basis. The trick is to follow a routine full of habits that reinforce this goal.

With that in mind, the premise of this book is simple: Hal and I will teach you how to not only take your personal life to the next level, we will also show you how to achieve a consistent word count and actually make money from your words.

If you want to attract, create, and sustain extraordinary levels of success and income, you must first figure out how to become the person that is capable of easily and consistently attracting, creating, and sustaining the extraordinary levels of success and income that you desire.

Beyond that, you also need to know how to build that consistent writing habit, achieve a flow state where the words fly on to the page, keep track of all your great ideas, and publish content through a business model that matches your personal style.

The Miracle Morning for Writers is different from other writing craft books because it combines nuts and bolts business tactics with strategies that improve your mental game. We won't simply tell you to "write thousands of words every day." Instead we show you how to make it happen, even when writing is the last thing you feel like doing.

It's Your Turn

What if you could wake up tomorrow morning with absolute faith that the day was going to be awesome? What if waking up early turned into a habit you absolutely loved? What if every morning could be like Christmas morning? You know, the really awesome Christmas mornings of your childhood when you went to bed full of anticipation for what was going to happen the next day and woke up so excited you woke your parents up at 4:00 a.m. to get on with the business of ripping open all of your gifts. (Or was that just me?) Any interest?

I can assure you that's exactly how I feel each and every day. I go to bed looking forward to the next day and wake up each morning anticipating what the day has in store for me. I'm grateful that I have transformed my life into something so amazing.

I know. You might be thinking, I've tried and failed. I've tried to get up earlier. I've tried to master my life and my professional growth. I have failed more times than I care to admit, and I'm nervous about trying something new. Can this really help me?

Yes it can!

I know what it's like to have that groggy feeling in the morning when you just don't feel like writing. But I now know what it's like to start a writing session energized and ready share my thoughts with the world. Trust me, it's a great feeling to start the afternoon knowing that my daily word count has already been completed. And that's what you'll learn how to do when you implement the information outlined in *The Miracle Morning for Writers*.

You can be just as successful, if not more so, than I have been.

All you have to do to start is take control of your morning.

Are you ready?

—1—
WHY MORNINGS MATTER
(MORE THAN YOU THINK)

How you start each morning determines your mindset, and the context, for the rest of your day. Start every day with a purposeful, disciplined, growth-infused, and goal-oriented morning, and you're virtually guaranteed to crush your day.

Yet most writers start their days with procrastination, hitting the snooze button, and sending the message to their subconscious that they don't have enough self-discipline to get out of bed in the morning, let alone do what's necessary to reach their writing goals.

When the alarm clock beeps in the morning, consider it to be akin to life's first gift to us. It's the gift of time to dedicate to becoming the person you need to be to achieve all of your goals and dreams while the rest of the world is still asleep.

You might be thinking, *All of this sounds great, Steve. But I am NOT a morning person.*

I understand. I really do! You're not saying anything I haven't told myself a thousand times before. And believe me, I tried—and failed—many times to take control of my mornings. But that was before I discovered the Miracle Morning.

Stay with me for a minute. In addition to becoming a successful writer, I bet you also want to stop struggling and worrying about your finances, quit missing your goals, and release all of the intense and not-so-great emotions that go along with those challenges. Am I right?

Then know this:

Mornings are the key to all of it.

More important than the time that you start your day is the mindset with which you start your day.

Maybe your dream is to become a famous writer so that you can inspect your alarm clock's insides with a baseball bat and see what it's like to start your day on your time for a while.

Trust me, I get it, and I often decide to start my day whenever I wake up naturally. However, even when I do that, my Miracle Morning is the first part of my day and gets me in the right mindset to make the most of the rest of my day.

Plus, there is a good chance that you are reading this book in the early stages of your author business, which means that you are probably paying your bills with a day job and writing on the side. If that's the case, then learning to implement your Miracle Morning routine with your day job is critical to exploding your writing efforts so that you can finally ditch that alarm clock for a few weekdays (or forever) and see how it feels. Here's the good news … It's worth it, and it is far more fun and rewarding than you might expect.

But, before we get into exactly how you can master your mornings, let me make the case for *why*. Because believe me, once you know the truth about mornings, you'll never want to miss one again.

Why Mornings Matter So Much

The more you dig into mornings, the more the proof mounts that the early bird gets a lot more than the worm. Here are just a few of the key advantages to laying off the snooze button.

You'll be more proactive. Christoph Randler is a professor of biology at the University of Education in Heidelberg, Germany. In the July 2010 issue of Harvard Business Review, Randler found that, "People whose performance peaks in the morning are better positioned for career success, because they're more proactive than people who are at their best in the evening."

You'll anticipate problems and head them off at the pass. Randler went on to surmise that morning people hold all of the important cards. They are "better able to anticipate and minimize problems, are proactive, have greater professional success and ultimately make higher wages." He noted that morning people are able to anticipate problems and handle them with grace and ease, which makes them better in business.

You'll plan like a pro. Morning folks have the time to organize, anticipate, and plan for their day. Our sleepy counterparts are reactive rather than proactive, leaving a lot to chance. Aren't you more stressed when you sleep through your alarm or wake up late? Getting up with the sun (or before) lets you jump-start the day. While everyone else is running around trying (and failing) to get their day under control, you'll be calm, cool, and collected.

You'll have more energy. One of the components of your new Miracle Mornings will be morning exercise, which—in as little as a few minutes a day—sets a positive tone for the day. Increased blood to the brain will help you think more clearly and focus on what's most important. Fresh oxygen will permeate every cell in your body and increase your energy all day, which is why successful writers who exercise report being in a better mood and in better shape, getting better sleep, and being more productive. This, of course, will result in your producing significant increases in your daily word count. You'll write more, publish more often, and earn more money from your writing.

You'll gain early bird attitude advantages ... Recently, researchers at the University of Barcelona in Spain, compared morning people, those early birds who like to get up at dawn, with evening people, night owls who prefer to stay up late and sleep in.

Among the differences, they found that morning people tend to be more persistent and resistant to fatigue, frustration, and difficulties. That translates into lower levels of anxiety and lower rates of depression, higher life satisfaction, and less likelihood of substance abuse. Sounds good to me.

... and you'll avoid night owl disadvantages. On the other hand, evening people tend to be more extravagant, temperamental, impulsive, and novelty-seeking, "with a higher tendency to explore the unknown." They are more likely to suffer from insomnia and ADHD. They also appear to be more likely to develop addictive behaviors, mental disorders, and antisocial tendencies—and even to attempt suicide. Not a pretty picture.

The evidence is in, and the experts have had their say. *Mornings contain the secret to an extraordinarily successful future with your writing career.*

Mornings? Really?

I'll admit it. To go from *I'm not a morning person* to *I really want to become a morning person* to *I'm up early every morning, and it's an awesome feeling!* is a process. But after some trial and error, you will discover how to out-fox, preempt, and foil your inner late sleeper so you can make early rising a habit. Okay, sounds great in theory, but you might be shaking your head and telling yourself, *There's no way. I'm already cramming 27 hours of stuff into 24 hours. How on earth could I get up an hour earlier than I already do?* I ask the question, how can you not?

The key thing to understand is that The Miracle Morning isn't about trying to deny yourself another hour of sleep so you can have an even longer, harder day. It's not even about waking up earlier. It's about waking up better.

Thousands of people around the planet are already living their own Miracle Mornings. Many of them were night owls. But they're making it work. In fact, they're thriving. And it's not because they added an hour to their day. It's because they added the right hour. And so can you.

Still skeptical? Then believe this: The hardest part about getting up an hour earlier is the first five minutes. That's the crucial time when, tucked into your warm bed, you make the decision to start your day or hit the snooze button just one more time. It's the moment of truth, and the decision you make right then will change your day, your success, and your life.

And that's why that first five minutes is the starting point for *The Miracle Morning for Writers*. It's time for you to win every morning!

In the next two chapters, I'll make waking up early easier and more exciting than it's ever been in your life (even if you've never considered yourself to be a morning person), and I'll show you how to maximize those newfound morning minutes.

Chapters 4, 5, and 6 will show you how to balance your Life S.AV.E.R.S., the specific components of your Miracle Morning, with the daily writing habit. Here, we dive into strategies you can use to overcome the obstacles that often get in the way of this routine, hitting a consistent word count, and managing every great book idea that comes to mind.

Finally, in chapters 7, 8, 9, and 10, I detail the process for becoming a professional writer. You'll learn how to create content that readers love, identify a writing business model that's perfect for you, and the eight-step strategy for building a writer platform where you can sell directly to your true fans.

There is a lot of information to cover, so let's dive into the content.

— 2 —

IT ONLY TAKES FIVE MINUTES TO BECOME A MORNING PERSON

I t is possible to love waking up—even if you've never been a morning person.

I know you might not believe it. Right now you may be thinking, *that might be true for early birds, but trust me, I've tried. I'm just not a morning person.*

But it's true. I know because I've been there. I was a bleary-eyed, snooze-button pusher. A "snooze-aholic" as Hal calls it. I was a morning dreader. I hated waking up.

And now I love it.

How did I do it? When people ask me how I transformed myself into a morning person—and transformed my life in the process—I tell them I did it in five simple steps, one at a time. I know it may seem downright impossible. But take it from a former snooze-aholic: you can do this. And you can do it the same way that I did.

That's the critical message about waking up: it's possible to change. Morning people aren't born—they're self-made. You can become a morning person, and you can do it in simple steps that don't require the willpower of an Olympic marathoner. I contend that when early rising becomes not something you do but who you are, you will truly love mornings. Waking up will become for you like it is for me, effortless.

Not convinced? Suspend your disbelief just a little and let me introduce you to the five-step process that changed my life. Five simple, snooze-proof keys that made waking up in the morning—even early in the morning—easier than ever before. Without this strategy, I would still be sleeping (or snoozing) through my alarm(s) each morning. Worse, I would still be clinging to the limiting belief that I was not a morning person.

And I would have missed a whole world of opportunity.

The Challenge with Waking Up

Waking up earlier is a bit like trying a new diet: It's easy to get pumped up about all the great results you're going to get, starting tomorrow.

But when tomorrow comes? And you're hungry? And your favorite food is staring up at you from the fridge or the café menu?

Well, we all know what happens then. Good intentions fly out the window. Motivation goes into hibernation. And the next thing you know, you're curled up with a tub of ice cream.

Mornings are not so different. Right now, I bet you're plenty motivated. But what happens tomorrow morning when that alarm goes off? How motivated will you be when you're yanked out of a deep sleep in a warm bed by a screaming alarm clock in a cold house?

I think we both know where your motivation will be right then. It will have gone off-shift and been replaced by rationalization. And rationalization is a crafty master—in just seconds we can convince ourselves that we need just a few extra minutes …

… and the next thing we know we're scrambling around the house late for work. And we haven't written one word either.

It's a tricky problem. Just when we need our motivation the most—those first few moments of the day—is precisely when we seem to have the least of it.

The solution, then, is to boost that morning motivation, to mount a surprise attack on rationalization. That's what the five steps that follow do. Each step in the process is designed to do one thing: increase what I call your Wake-Up Motivation Level (WUML).

First thing in the morning, you might have a low WUML, meaning you want nothing more than to go back to sleep when your alarm goes off. That's normal. But by using this process, you can reach a high WUML where you're ready to jump up and embrace the day.

The Five-Minute Snooze-Proof Wake-Up Strategy

Minute One: Set Your Intentions before Bed

The first key to waking up is to remember this: Your first thought in the morning is usually the last thought you had before you went to bed. I bet, for example, that you've had nights where you could hardly fall asleep because you were so excited about waking up the next morning. Whether it was Christmas morning or the start of a big vacation, as soon as the alarm clock sounded you opened your eyes ready to jump out of bed and embrace the day. Why? It's because the last thought you had about the coming morning before you went to bed was positive.

On the other hand, if your last thought before bed was something like, Oh man, I can't believe I have to get up in six hours— I'm going to be exhausted in the morning! then your first thought when the alarm clock goes off is likely to be something like, Oh my gosh, it's already been six hours? Nooo! I just want to keep sleeping!

The first step, then, is to consciously decide every night to actively and mindfully create a positive expectation for the next morning.

For help on this and to get the precise words to say before bed to create your powerful intentions, download *The Miracle Morning Bedtime Affirmations* for free at www.TMMBook.com.

Minute Two: Walk *Across the Room* to Turn off The Alarm

If you haven't already, move your alarm clock across the room. This forces you to get out of bed and engage your body in movement. Motion creates energy—getting all the way up and out of bed naturally helps you wake up.

If you keep your alarm clock next to your bed, you're still in a partial sleep state when the alarm goes off, and it makes it much more difficult to wake yourself up. In fact, you may have turned off the alarm without even realizing it! On more than a few occasions, you might have even convinced yourself that your alarm clock was merely part of the dream you were having. (You're not alone on that one; trust me.)

Simply forcing yourself to get out of bed to turn off the alarm clock will instantly increase your WUML. However, you'll likely still be feeling more sleepy than not. So to raise that WUML just a little further, try …

Minute Three: Brush Your Teeth

As soon as you've gotten out of bed and turned off your alarm clock, go directly to the bathroom sink to brush your teeth. While you're at it, splash some water on your face. This simple activity will increase your WUML even further.

Now that your mouth is fresh, it's time to …

Minute Four: Drink a Full Glass of Water

It's crucial that you hydrate yourself first thing every morning. After six to eight hours without water, you'll be mildly dehydrated, which causes fatigue. Often when people feel tired—at any time of the day—what they really need is more water, not more sleep.

Start by getting a glass or bottle of water (or you can do what I do, and fill it up the night before so it's already there for you in the morning), and drink it as fast as is comfortable for you. The objective is to replace the water you were deprived of during the hours you slept. (And hey, the side benefits of morning hydration are better, younger-looking skin and even maintaining a healthy weight. Not bad for a few ounces of water!)

That glass of water should raise your WUML another notch, which will get you to ...

Minute Five: Get Dressed or Jump in the Shower

The fifth step has two options. Option one is to get dressed in your exercise clothes, so you're ready to leave your bedroom and immediately engage in your *Miracle Morning*. You can either lay out your clothes before you go to bed or even sleep in your work-out clothes. (Yes, really.)

Option two is to jump in the shower. I usually change into exercise clothes since I'll need a shower after working out, but a lot of people prefer the morning shower because it helps them wake up and gives them a fresh start to the day. The choice is yours.

Regardless of which option you choose, by the time you've executed these five simple steps, your WUML should be high enough that it requires very little discipline to stay awake for your *Miracle Morning*.

If you were to try and make that commitment at the moment your alarm clock first went off—while you were at a WUML of nearly zero—it would be a much more difficult decision to make. The five steps let you build momentum so that within just a few minutes you're ready to go instead of feeling groggy.

Miracle Morning Bonus Wake-Up Tips

Although this strategy has worked for thousands of people, these five steps are not the only way to make waking up in the morning easier. Here are a few other tips I've heard from fellow Miracle Morning practitioners:

The Miracle Morning "Bedtime Affirmations": If you haven't done this yet, be sure to take a moment now to go to www.TMMbook.com and download the re-energizing, intention-setting "Bedtime Affirmations" for free. There is nothing more effective for ensuring you will wake up before your alarm than programming your mind to achieve exactly what you want.

Set a timer for your bedroom lights: One of The Miracle Morning Community members sets his bedroom lights on a timer (you can buy an appliance timer online or at your local hardware store). As his alarm goes off, the lights come on in the room. What a great idea! It's a lot easier to fall back asleep when it's dark—having the lights on tells your mind and body that it's time to wake up. (Regardless of whether you use a timer, be sure to turn your light on first thing when your alarm goes off.)

Set a timer for your bedroom heater: Another fan of The Miracle Morning says that in the winter, she keeps a bedroom heater on an appliance timer set to go off fifteen minutes before she wakes up. She keeps it cold at night but warm for waking up so that she won't be tempted to crawl back under her covers.

Feel free to add to or customize the Five-Minute Snooze-Proof Wake-Up Strategy, and if you have any tips you're open to sharing, we'd love to hear them. Please share them in The Miracle Morning Community at www.MyTMMCommunity.com.

Waking up consistently and easily is all about having an effective, pre-determined, step-by-step strategy to increase your WUML in the morning. Don't wait to try this! Start tonight by reading The Miracle Morning "Bedtime Affirmations," moving your alarm clock across the room, setting a glass of water on your nightstand, and committing to the other two steps for the morning.

How to Go from Unbearable to Unstoppable (In 30 Days)

Incorporating any new habit requires an adjustment period—don't expect this to be effortless from day one. But do make a commitment to yourself to stick with it. The seemingly unbearable first few days are only temporary. While there's a lot of debate around how long it takes to create a new habit, 30 days is definitely enough to test-drive your new morning routine.

Here's what you might expect as you build your new routine.

Phase One: Unbearable (Days 1–10)

Phase One is when any new activity requires tremendous effort, and getting up early is no different. You're fighting existing habits, the very habits that have been entrenched in who you are for years.

In this phase, it's mind over matter—and if you don't mind, it'll definitely matter! The habits of hitting snooze and not making the most of your day are the same habits that are holding you back from becoming the prolific writer you have always known you could be, so dig in and hold strong.

In Phase One, while you battle existing patterns and limiting beliefs, you'll find out what you're made of and what you're capable of. You need to keep pushing, stay committed to your vision, and hang in there. Trust me when I say you can do this!

I know it can be daunting on day five to realize you still have twenty-five days to go before your transformation is complete and you've become a bona fide morning person. Keep in mind that on day five, you're actually more than halfway through the first phase and well on your way. Remember: Your initial feelings are not going to last forever. In fact, you owe it to yourself to persevere because, in no time at all, you'll be getting the exact results you want as you become the person you've always wanted to be!

Phase Two: Uncomfortable (Days 11–20)

In Phase Two, your body and mind begin to acclimate to waking up earlier. You'll notice that getting up earlier starts to get a tiny bit easier, but it's not yet a habit—it's not quite who you are and likely won't feel natural yet.

The biggest temptation at this level is to reward yourself by taking a break, especially on the weekends. A question posted quite often in The Miracle Morning Community is, "How many days a week do you get up early for your Miracle Morning?" My answer—and the one that's most common from long-time Miracle Morning practitioners—is *every single day*.

Once you've made it through Phase One, you've made it through the hardest period. So keep going! Why on earth would you want to go through that first phase again by taking one or two days off? Trust me, you wouldn't, so don't!

Phase Three: Unstoppable (Days 21–30)

Early rising is now not only a habit, it has literally become part of *who you are*, part of your identity. Your body and mind will have become accustomed to your new way of being. These next ten days are important for cementing the habit in yourself and your life.

As you engage in the Miracle Morning practice, you will also develop an appreciation for the three distinct phases of habit change. A side benefit is you will realize that you can identify, develop, and adopt any habit that serves you—up to and including the habits of the top performers I have included in this book.

What Do I DO With My Morning?

Thirty days, you might be thinking, *I can get up earlier for thirty days ... But what do I DO with that time?*

This is where the magic begins. I'm going to introduce you to the routines at the heart of *The Miracle Morning*. They're called the Life S.A.V.E.R.S., and they're the habits that are going to transform your mornings, your career, and your life!

Taking Immediate Action:

There's no need to wait to get started with creating your new, amazing future. As Anthony Robbins has said, "When is NOW a good time for you to do that? Now, indeed, would be perfect!" In fact, the sooner you start, the sooner you'll begin to see results, including increased energy, a better attitude, and of course, more success with your writing.

Step One: Set your alarm for one hour earlier than you usually wake up, and schedule that hour in your calendar to do your first Miracle Morning ... tomorrow morning.

From this day forward, starting with the next 30 days, keep your alarm set for 60 minutes earlier to start waking up when you want to, instead of when you have to. It's time to launch each day with a Miracle Morning so that you can become the person you need to be to be a successful author.

What will you do with that hour? We're going to find out in the next chapter, but for now, simply continue reading this book during your Miracle Morning until you learn the whole routine.

Step Two: Join The Miracle Morning Community at www. MyTMMCommunity.com to connect with and get additional support from more than 40,000 like-minded early risers, many of whom have been generating extraordinary results with The Miracle Morning for years.

Step Three: Find a Miracle Morning accountability partner. Enroll someone—a friend, family member, or a fellow writer—to join you on this adventure and hold each other accountable to follow through until your Miracle Morning has become part of you.

— 3 —
THE LIFE S.A.V.E.R.S.
SIX PRACTICES GUARANTEED TO SAVE YOU FROM A LIFE OF UNFULFILLED POTENTIAL

When Hal experienced the second of his two self-proclaimed rock bottoms, both of which you can read about in *The Miracle Morning*, he began his own quest for the fastest way to take his personal development to the next level. So, he went in search of the daily practices of the world's most successful people.

After discovering six of the most proven, timeless personal development practices, Hal first attempted to determine which one or two would accelerate his success the fastest. Then he asked himself, *what would happen if I did ALL of them?*

He transformed his life after discovering, implementing, and mastering those practices, which he came to call the Life S.A.V.E.R.S. But it wasn't just him. Countless others adopt the Life S.A.V.E.R.S. and transform themselves, too. And I soon followed.

Why the Life S.A.V.E.R.S. Work

The Life S.A.V.E.R.S. are simple but profoundly effective daily morning practices that help you plan and live your life on your terms. They're designed to start your day in a peak physical, mental, emotional, and spiritual state so that you both continually improve and will ALWAYS perform at your best.

What you need to realize right now is that your Miracle Morning will create time for you. The Life S.A.V.E.R.S. are the vehicle to help you stop working harder and longer and begin working smarter and more efficiently instead. The practices help you build energy, see priorities more clearly, and find the stress-free productive flow in your life.

In other words, the Life S.A.V.E.R.S. don't take more time from your day but ultimately add more to it.

Each letter in S.A.V.E.R.S. represents one of the best practices of the most successful people on the planet. And they're also the same activities that bring new levels of peace, clarity, motivation, and energy to your life. They are:

Silence

Affirmations

Visualization

Exercise

Reading

Scribing

These practices are the best possible use of your newfound morning time. They're customizable to fit you, your life, and your goals. And you can start first thing tomorrow morning.

Let's go through each of the six practices in detail.

S is for Silence

Silence, the first practice of the Life S.A.V.E.R.S., is a key habit. If you're surrounded by the endless barrage of phone calls, emails, meetings, and deadlines, then this is your opportunity to STOP and BREATHE!

Most people start the day by checking email, texts, and social media. And most people struggle to be successful. It's not a coincidence. Starting each day with a period of silence instead will immediately reduce your stress levels and help you begin the day with the kind of calm and clarity that you need in order to focus on what's most important.

Many of the most successful people in the world, in every industry, are daily practitioners of silence. It's not surprising that Oprah practices stillness—or that she does nearly all of the other Life S.A.V.E.R.S. too. Musicians Katy Perry and Russell Brand practice transcendental meditation, as do Sheryl Crow and Sir Paul McCartney. Film and television stars Jennifer Aniston, Ellen Degeneres, Jerry Seinfeld, Howard Stern, Cameron Diaz, Clint Eastwood, and Hugh Jackman have all spoken of their daily meditation practices. Even famous billionaires Ray Dalio and Rupert Murdoch have attributed their financial success to practicing stillness on a daily basis. You'll be in good (and quiet) company by doing the same.

If it seems like I'm asking you to simply do nothing, let me clarify: you have a number of choices for your practice of silence. In no particular order, here are a few to get you started:

- Meditation
- Prayer
- Reflection
- Deep breathing
- Gratitude

Whichever you choose, be sure you don't stay in bed for your period of silence, and better still, get out of your bedroom altogether.

The Benefits of Silence

How many times do we find ourselves in stressful situations? How many times are we dealing with immediate obstacles that take us away from our writing routine? No, those aren't trick questions—the answer is the same for both: every single day. Stress is one of the most common reasons that writers lose focus. Daily, I face the ever-present distractions of other people encroaching on my schedule and the inevitable fires I must extinguish. Quieting the mind allows me to put those things aside and focus on working on my writing business instead of reacting to the latest distraction that crosses my path.

But the effect goes beyond productivity. Excessive stress is terrible for your health, too. It triggers your fight-or-flight response, and that releases a cascade of toxic hormones that can stay in your body for days. That's fine if you experience that type of stress only occasionally. But when the constant barrage of a life as a writer keeps the adrenaline flowing all the time, the negative impact on your health adds up.

Silence in the form of meditation, however, can reduce stress, and as a result, improve your health. A major study run by several groups, including the National Institutes of Health, the American Medical Association, the Mayo Clinic, and scientists from both Harvard and Stanford, stated that meditation can reduce stress and high blood pressure. A recent study by Dr. Norman Rosenthal, a world-renowned psychiatrist who works with the David Lynch Foundation, even found that people who practice meditation are 30 percent less likely to die from heart disease.

Another study from Harvard found that just eight weeks of meditation could lead to "increased grey-matter density in the hippocampus, known to be important for learning and memory, and in structures associated with self-awareness, compassion and introspection."

Practicing silence, in other words, can help you reduce your stress, improve cognitive performance, and replace medication with meditation at the same time.

Guided Meditations and Meditation Apps

Meditation is like anything else—if you've never done it before, then it can be difficult or feel awkward at first. If you are a first time meditator, I recommend starting with a guided meditation.

Here are a few of my favorite meditation apps that are available for both iPhone/iPad and Android devices:

- Headspace
- Calm
- Omvana
- Simply Being

There are both subtle and significant differences among these meditation apps, one of which is the voice of the person speaking.

If you don't have a device that allows you to download apps, simply go to YouTube or Google and search on the keywords "Guided Meditation."

Miracle Morning (Individual) Meditation

When you're ready to try an unguided meditation, here is a simple, step-by-step meditation you can use during your Miracle Morning, even if you've never meditated before.

- Before beginning your meditation, it's important to prepare your mindset and set your expectations. This is a time for you to quiet your mind and let go of the compulsive need to constantly be thinking about something—reliving the past or worrying about the future, but never living fully in the present. This is the time to let go of your stresses, take a break from worrying about your problems, and be fully present in this moment. It is a time to access the essence of who you truly are—to go deeper than what you have, what you do, or the labels you've accepted as who you are. If this sounds foreign to you, or too new age, that's okay. I've felt the same way. It's probably because you've never tried it before. But thankfully, you're about to.

- Find a quiet, comfortable place to sit. You can sit up straight on the couch, on a chair, on the floor, or on a pillow for added comfort.

- Sit upright, cross-legged. You can close your eyes, or you can look down at a point on the ground about two feet in front of you.

- Begin by focusing on your breath, taking slow, deep breaths. Breathe in through the nose and out through the mouth. The most effective breathing causes your belly to expand and not your chest.

- Now start pacing your breath; breathe in slowly for a count of three seconds (one one thousand, two one thousand, three one thousand), hold it in for another three counts, and then breathe out slowly for a final count of three. Feel your thoughts and emotions settling down as you focus on your breath. Be aware that, as you attempt to quiet your mind, thoughts will still come in to pay a visit. Simply acknowledge them, and then let them go, always returning your focus to your breath.

- Try being fully present in this moment. This is often referred to as just being. Not thinking, not doing, just being. Continue to follow your breath, and imagine inhaling positive, loving and peaceful energy, and exhaling all of your worries and stress. Enjoy the quiet. Enjoy the moment. Just breathe … Just be.

- If you find that you have a constant influx of thoughts, it may be helpful for you to focus on a single word, phrase, or mantra and repeat it over and over again to yourself as you inhale and exhale. For example, you might try something like this: (On the inhale) "I inhale confidence …" (As you exhale) "I exhale fear …" You can swap the word confidence for whatever you feel you need to bring more of into your life (love, faith, energy, etc.), and swap the word fear with whatever you feel you need to let go of (stress, worry, resentment, etc.).

Meditation is a gift you can give yourself every day. My time spent meditating has become one of my favorite parts of the routine. It's a time to be at peace and to experience gratitude and freedom from my day-to-day stressors and worries.

Think of daily meditation as a temporary vacation from your problems. While your problems will still be there when you finish your daily meditation, you'll find that you're much more centered and better equipped to solve them.

A is for Affirmations

Have you ever wondered why some people are more successful than others? Time and time again, I notice that mindset is a driving factor in performance.

Those around you can sense your mindset. It shows up undeniably in your language, your confidence, and your demeanor.

I know firsthand, though, how difficult it can be for writers to maintain confidence and enthusiasm—not to mention motivation—during the rollercoaster ride of publishing content. Mindset is largely something we adopt without conscious thought. At a subconscious level, we have all been programmed to think, believe, act, and talk to ourselves a certain way. When times get tough, we revert to our habitual, programmed mindset.

Our programming has come from many influences, including what we've have been told by others, what we've told ourselves, and all of our good and bad life experiences. That programming expresses itself throughout our lives, including in our writing. And that means if we want to get better at writing, we need better mental programming.

Affirmations are a tool for doing just that. By repeatedly telling yourself who you want to be, what you want to accomplish, and how you are going to accomplish it, your subconscious mind will shift your beliefs and behavior. You'll automatically believe and act in new ways, and eventually manifest your affirmations into your reality.

Science has proven that affirmations—when done correctly—are one of the most effective tools for quickly becoming the person you need to be to achieve everything you want in your life. And yet, affirmations sometimes get a bad rap. Many have tried them only to be disappointed with little or no results.

Why the Old Way of Doing Affirmations Doesn't Work

For decades, countless so-called experts and gurus have taught affirmations in ways that have proven to be ineffective and set people up for failure, time and time again. Here are two of the most common problems with affirmations.

Lying to Yourself Doesn't Work

I am a millionaire. No, you're not.

I have 7 percent body fat. No, you don't.

I have achieved all of my goals this year. Nope. Sorry, you haven't.

This method of creating affirmations that are written as if you've already become or achieved something may be the single biggest reason that affirmations haven't worked for most people.

With this technique, every time you recite an affirmation that simply isn't rooted in truth, your subconscious will resist it. As an intelligent human being who isn't delusional, lying to yourself repeatedly will never be the optimum strategy. The truth will always prevail.

Passive Language Doesn't Produce Results

Many affirmations have been designed to make you feel good by creating an empty promise of something you desire. For example, here is a popular money affirmation that's been perpetuated for decades, by many world-famous gurus:

I am a money magnet. Money flows to me effortlessly and in abundance.

This type of affirmation might make you feel good in the moment by giving you a false sense of relief from your financial worries, but it won't generate any income. People who sit back and wait for money to magically show up are cash poor.

To generate financial abundance (or any result you desire, for that matter), you've got to actually do something. Your actions must be in alignment with your desired results, and your affirmations must articulate and affirm both.

4 Steps to Create Affirmations That Improve Your Writing Business

Here are simple steps for creating and implementing results-oriented Miracle Morning affirmations, which will program both your conscious and subconscious mind to produce results and take your levels of personal and writing success beyond what you've ever experienced before.

Step 1: The Extraordinary Result You Are Committed to and Why

Notice I'm not starting with "What you want." Everyone wants things, but we don't get what we want; we get what we're committed to. You want to write a book? Who cares; join that nonexclusive club. Oh wait, you're 100 percent committed to writing a book by creating a consistent writing habit? Okay, now we're talking.

Action: Start by writing down a (specific) extraordinary result or outcome—one that challenges you and would significantly improve your life and one that you are ready to commit to creating (even if you're not yet sure how you will do it). Then, reinforce your commitment by including your WHY, the compelling benefits that you'll get to experience.

Examples: I am committed to doubling my writing income in the next 12 months, from $_____ to $_____, so that I can provide additional financial security for my family.

Or ...

I am 100 percent committed to writing _____ words by _____ (date) so that I'll have completed the rough draft of my book.

Step 2: The Necessary Actions You Are Committed to Taking and When

Writing an affirmation that merely affirms what you want without affirming what you are committed to doing is one step above pointless and can actually be counterproductive by tricking your subconscious mind into thinking that the result will happen automatically without effort.

Action: Clarify the (specific) action, activity, or habit that is required for you to achieve your writing goal and clearly state WHEN and how often you will execute the necessary action.

Examples: To guarantee that I double my writing income, I am committed to doubling my daily word count from 1,000 words to 2,000 words five days a week from 7:00 a.m. to 9:00 a.m.—NO MATTER WHAT HAPPENS DURING THE REST OF THE DAY!

Or …

To ensure that I finish the rough draft of my book by_____ (date), I am 100 percent committed to writing for 60 minutes each day from 6:00 a.m. to 7:00 a.m.

The more specific your actions are, the better. Be sure to include frequency (how often), quantity (how many), and precise time frames (which times you will begin and end your activities).

Step 3: Recite Your Affirmations Every Morning with Emotion

Remember, your Miracle Morning affirmations aren't designed merely to make you feel good. These are written statements that are strategically engineered to program your subconscious mind with the beliefs and overall mindset you need to achieve your desired outcomes while directing your conscious mind to keep you focused on your highest priorities and taking the actions that will get you there.

In order for your affirmations to be effective, it is important that you tap into your emotions while reciting them. Mindlessly repeating an affirmation over and over again, without intentionally feeling its truth, will have minimal impact for you. You must take responsibility for generating authentic emotions, such as excitement and determination, and powerfully infusing those emotions into every affirmation you recite.

Action: Schedule time each day to read your affirmations in the morning (ideally during your Miracle Morning) to both program your subconscious and focus your conscious mind on what's most important to you and what you are committed to doing to make it your reality. That's right, you must read them daily. Reading an occasional affirmation is as effective as getting an occasional work-out. You'll start seeing results only once you've made them a part of your daily routine.

Step 4: Constantly Update and Evolve Your Affirmations

As you continue to grow, improve, and evolve, so should your affirmations. When you come up with a new goal, dream, or any extraordinary result that you want to create for your life, add it to your affirmations.

Personally, I have affirmations for every significant area of my life (finances, health, happiness, relationships, parenting, etc.), and I am constantly updating my affirmations as I learn more. I stay on the lookout for quotes, strategies, and philosophies that I can add to improve my mindset. Any time you come across an empowering quote or philosophy and think, *that is a huge area of improvement for me,* add it to your affirmations.

Your programming can be changed and improved at any time starting right now. You can reprogram any perceived limitations with new beliefs and behaviors so you can become as successful as you want to be in any area of life you choose.

In summary, your new affirmations will articulate which extraordinary results you are committed to creating, why they are critically important to you, and, most importantly, which necessary actions you are committed to taking, and precisely when you are committed to taking them, to ensure that you attain and sustain the extraordinary levels of success that you truly want (and deserve) for your life.

Affirmations to Become a Prolific Writer

In addition to the formula to create your affirmations, I have included this list of sample affirmations that prolific writers use regularly to increase growth and productivity and improve in different areas of their business. Feel free to include any of these that resonate with you.

- I dedicate time each day to creating content that will both educate and entertain my readers.

- Rejection and negative reviews are a normal part of the publishing process. I will do my best to learn from the constructive critiques, but I never let the haters bring me down.

- I leave every interaction with my fans and followers energized because they appreciate my work and look forward to my next writing project.

- ✗ Building a writing business isn't about me and what I want; it is about connecting with readers, giving them what they want, and doing my best to positively impact their lives.

- Writer's block is no match for me! I always come up with compelling plot lines and powerful narratives whenever I'm about to write.

- I commit to writing a minimum of ___ words Monday through Friday between ___:___ a.m./p.m. and ___:___ a.m./p.m., no matter what.

- ✗ I focus on learning new things and improving my writing craft daily, and I commit to reading at least one or two new books every month.

- ✗ The secret to successful writing is to commit to my daily process without being emotionally attached to the outcome. I can't always control my results, but as long as I follow through with the process, the law of averages will always play out, and my outcomes will take care of themselves.

These are just a few examples of affirmations. You can use any of these that resonate with you or create your own using the four-step formula described in the previous pages. Anything you repeat to yourself over and over again with emotion will be programmed into your subconscious mind, form new beliefs, and manifest itself through your actions.

V is for Visualization

Visualization is a technique for using your imagination to create what you want in life.

Visualization is a well-known habit of top athletes, who use it to enhance their performance. Olympic athletes and top performers in many categories incorporate visualization as a critical part of their daily training. What is less well known is that other successful people use it just as frequently.

If you'd like some fascinating information on why visualization works, just Google "mirror neurons." Mirror neurons are a relatively new area of study in neurology, and they seem to allow us to improve our abilities not only by watching other people perform them, but also by visualizing ourselves performing them. Some studies indicate that experienced weight lifters can increase muscle mass through vivid visualization sessions, and mirror neurons are the reason why this is possible. In many ways, the brain can't tell the difference between a vivid visualization and the actual experience. Crazy, right?

I had always been a little skeptical about the value of visualization because it sounded a little too new agey. Once I read about mirror neurons, my whole attitude changed!

What Do You Visualize?

Many people are limited by visions of their past results, replaying previous failures and heartbreaks. Creative visualization, on the other hand, enables you to design a new vision that will occupy your mind, ensuring that the greatest pull on you is your future—a compelling, exciting, and limitless future.

After I've read my affirmations, I sit upright, close my eyes, and take a few slow, deep breaths. For the next five to ten minutes, I simply visualize the specific actions that are necessary to make my long- and short-term goals a reality.

Notice that I did not say that I visualize the results. Many people will disagree on this issue, but there are some studies that show that visualizing the victory (for example, standing on stage, driving the car, moving into the house, hiring the new team member, etc.) can actually diminish your drive because your brain has already experienced the reward on some level. Instead, I would recommend using visualization as a practice session for improving the skills or aspects of your life that you are working on. Visualize actions, not results.

As a writer, you might picture yourself working hard on a book. Think of the perfect scenario that leads to creating something your readers will love. Picture all the great ideas surfacing in your head and the diligent research you complete for the next project. Then imagine what it's like to write the book. How would this look? Are you thoroughly covering the content in your beats or outline? What are you doing to prevent writer's block? Are you trusting that your editor will fix those small mistakes, so you can get your thoughts down fast?

The key to this visualization exercise is to take full responsibility for your actions—instead of agonizing over outcomes that are beyond your control. By walking yourself through the perfect writing process, you will identify all the steps you need to complete and what needs to be done to make them happen!

3 Simple Steps for Miracle Morning Visualization

Directly after reading your affirmations is the perfect time to visualize yourself living in alignment with them.

Step 1: Get Ready

Some people like to play instrumental music in the background, such as classical or baroque (check out anything from the composer J.S. Bach), during their visualization. If you'd like to experiment with playing music, put it on with the volume relatively low. Personally, I find anything with words to be a distraction.

Now, sit up tall in a comfortable position. This can be on a chair, the couch, or the floor. Breathe deeply. Close your eyes, clear your mind, and get ready to visualize.

Step 2: Visualize What You Really Want

The greatest gift you can give to the people you love is to live up to your full potential. What does that look like for you? What do you really want? Forget about logic, limits, and being practical. If you could have anything you wanted, do anything you wanted, and be anything you wanted, what would you choose? What specific actions would you have to do to get it? What would you have to become? How would you act in different situations?

See, feel, hear, touch, taste, and smell every detail of your vision. Involve all of your senses to maximize the effectiveness of your visualization. The more vivid you make your vision, the more compelled you'll be to take the necessary actions to make it a reality.

Step 3: Visualize Who You Need To Be and What You Need To Do

Once you've created a clear mental picture of what you want, begin to visualize yourself living in total alignment with the person you need to be to achieve your vision. See yourself engaged in the positive actions you'll need to do each day (exercising, studying, working, writing, making calls, sending emails, etc.) and make sure you see yourself enjoying the process. See yourself smiling as you're running on that treadmill, filled with a sense of pride for your self-discipline to follow through.

Imagine yourself coming up with great ideas on a daily basis, crafting outlines that detail every aspect of your book, flying through your first draft then carefully tweaking the copy in the second and third drafts. Then you can visualize what it's like to publish this book and make that one-on-one connection with a reader. What is it like to both educate and entertain this person? Think of every aspect of the publishing process and create a mental movie of how you'd perfectly manage each step in the process.

Final Thoughts on Visualization

When you combine reading your affirmations every morning with daily visualization, you will turbocharge the programming of your subconscious mind for success. You will begin to live in alignment with your ideal vision and make it a reality. When you visualize daily, you align your thoughts and feelings with your vision. This makes it easier to maintain the motivation you need to continue taking the necessary actions. Visualization can be a powerful aid in overcoming self-limiting habits, such as procrastination, and in taking the actions necessary to achieve your goals.

E is for Exercise

Exercise should be a staple of your Miracle Morning. Even a few minutes of exercise each morning significantly enhances your health, improves your self-confidence and emotional well-being, and enables you to think better and concentrate longer. You'll also notice how quickly your energy level increases with daily exercise, and your clients will notice it, too—even over the phone.

Personal development experts and self-made multi-millionaire entrepreneurs Eben Pagan and Tony Robbins (who is also a best-selling author) both agree that the number one key to success is to start every morning off with a personal success ritual. Included in both of their success rituals is some type of morning exercise. If it's good enough for Eben and Tony, it's good enough for me.

Lest you think you have to engage in triathlon or marathon training, think again. Your morning exercise also doesn't need to replace an afternoon or evening regimen, if you already have one in place. You can still hit the gym after you've reached your daily word count or edited your latest blog. However, the benefits from adding as little as five minutes of morning exercise are undeniable, including improved blood pressure and blood sugar levels and decreased risk of all kinds of scary things like heart disease, osteoporosis, cancer, and diabetes. Maybe most importantly, a little exercise in the morning will increase your energy levels for the rest of the day.

You can go for a walk or run, hit the gym, throw on a P90X or Insanity DVD, watch a yoga video on YouTube, or find a Life S.A.V.E.R.S. buddy to play some early morning racquetball. There's also an excellent app called 7 Minute Workout that give you a full body workout in—you guessed it—seven minutes. The choice is yours—just pick one and do it.

Unfortunately, writing is an extremely sedentary activity. So you need to be more active than most people and make sure that 30 minutes of additional exercise is scheduled in your daily routine.

Exercise for Your Brain

Even if you don't care about your physical health, consider that exercise is simply going to make you smarter, and that can only help your writing. Dr. Steven Masley, a Florida physician and nutritionist with a health practice geared toward executives, explains how exercise creates a direct connection to your cognitive ability.

"If we're talking about brain performance, the best predictor of brain speed is aerobic capacity—how well you can run up a hill is very strongly correlated with brain speed and cognitive shifting ability," Masley said.

Masley has designed a corporate wellness program based on the work he's done with more than 1,000 patients. "The average person going into these programs will increase brain speed by 25–30 percent."

Imagine how a 25-30 percent increase in brain speed could improve your writing ability. How many great thoughts would you have? What would it be like to think of additional publishing opportunities that you might not have originally considered? What would your state of mind be? How different would you feel? What might that do for the success of your writing business?

Hal chose yoga and began practicing it shortly after he created the Miracle Morning. He's been doing it and loving it ever since. My exercise routine is a daily practice where I either go for run while listening to great podcasts or walk around my neighborhood with my wife. Or even both in the same day. This accomplishes several things at once: the run helps to wake me up and get my Miracle Morning started, I get a dose of vitamin D for my mind and body, and I get a dose of inspiration from whatever I may be listening to.

My recommendation is to find what resonates with you and make it a part of your Miracle Morning.

Final Thoughts on Exercise

You know that if you want to maintain good health and increase your energy you must exercise consistently. That's not news to anyone. But what also isn't news is how easy it is to make excuses. Two of the biggest are "I don't have time" and "I'm too tired." There is no limit to the excuses that you can think of. And the more creative you are, the more excuses you can come up with!

That's the beauty of incorporating exercise into your Miracle Morning—it happens before your day wears you out and before you have an entire day to come up with new excuses. Because it happens first, the Miracle Morning is a surefire way to avoid all of those excuses and to make exercise a daily habit.

Legal disclaimer: Hopefully this goes without saying, but you should consult your doctor or physician before beginning any exercise regimen, especially if you are experiencing any physical pain, discomfort, disabilities, etc. You may need to modify or even refrain from your exercise routine to meet your individual needs.

R is for Reading

One of the fastest ways to achieve everything you want is to model successful people. For every goal you have, there's a good chance that an expert out there has already achieved the same thing, or something similar. As Tony Robbins has said, "Success leaves clues."

Fortunately, some of the best of the best have shared their stories throughout history in the form of writing. And that means all those success blueprints are just waiting out there for anyone willing to invest some time in reading. Books are a limitless supply of help and mentorship right at your fingertips.

Occasionally, I'll hear somebody say, "I'm just not a big reader." I get it. I used to have that attitude as well. I think back to what my mentor used to say: "The greatest minds of our time and in human history have spent years, and sometimes decades, to condense the best of what they know into a few pages that can be read in a few hours and purchased for a few dollars ... but you're not a big reader. That's a bad decision." Ouch!

Want to come up with great book ideas? Looking to improve your writing skills? Hoping to turn your writing into a profitable business? Then be a reader!

Here are some of my favorites that will specifically help you in the areas of writing and developing your skills. These are not good books. These are great books that will significantly impact you if you let them.

On the Craft of Writing:

- ✔ *The Story Grid: What Good Editors Know* by Shawn Coyne
- ✔ *The Elements of Style* by William Strunk Jr. and E. B. White
- ✔ *2K to 10K: Writing Faster, Writing Better, and Writing More of What You Love* by Rachel Aaron
- ✔ *On Writing: A Memoir of the Craft* by Stephen King
- ✔ *Take Off Your Pants! Outline Your Books for Faster, Better Writing* by Libbie Hawker
- *You Are a Writer (So Start Acting Like One)* by Jeff Goins
- *Prosperity for Writers: A Writer's Guide to Creating Abundance* by Honorée Corder
- *The Artist's Way* by Julia Cameron
- *The War of Art: Break Through the Blocks and Win Your Inner Creative Battles* by Steven Pressfield
- ✔ *Business for Authors: How To Be An Author Entrepreneur* by Joanna Penn
- *On Writing Well: The Classic Guide to Writing Nonfiction* by William Zinsser
- *Writing Tools: 50 Essential Strategies for Every Writer* by Roy Peter Clark

On Mindset:

✓ *The One Thing: The Surprisingly Simple Truth Behind Extraordinary Results* by Gary Keller and Jay Papasan

✓ *The Art of Exceptional Living* by Jim Rohn

✓ *Vision to Reality: How Short Term Massive Action Equals Long Term Maximum Results* by Honorée Corder

✓ *The 7 Habits of Highly Effective People: Powerful Lessons in Personal Change* by Stephen R. Covey

✓ *Essentialism: The Disciplined Pursuit of Less* by Greg Mckeown

✓ *Mastery* by Robert Greene

✓ *The Success Principles: How to Get from Where You Are to Where You Want to Be* by Jack Canfield and Janet Switzer

✓ *The Game of Life and How to Play It* by Florence Scovel Shinn

✓ *The Compound Effect* by Darren Hardy

• *Taking Life Head On: How to Love the Life You Have While You Create the Life of Your Dreams* by Hal Elrod

✓ *Think and Grow Rich* by Napoleon Hill

In addition to finding writing success, you can transform your relationships, increase your self-confidence, improve your communication or persuasion skills, learn how to become healthy, and improve any other area of your life you can think of. Head to your local bookstore—or do what I do and visit Amazon.com—and you'll find more books than you can possibly imagine on any area of your life you want to improve.

For a complete list of Hal's favorite personal development books, including those that have made the biggest impact on his success and happiness, check out the Recommended Reading list at www.TMMBook.com.

How Much Should You Read?

I recommend committing to read a minimum of ten pages per day (although five is okay to start with if you read slowly or don't yet enjoy reading).

Ten pages does not seem like much, but let's do the math. Reading ten pages a day gives you 3,650 pages a year. That stacks up to approximately eighteen 200-page personal development or self-improvement books! And all of that will happen in 10-15 minutes of reading or 15-30 minutes if you read more slowly.

Let me ask you, if you read 18 personal development or success books in the next year, do you think you'd be more knowledgeable, capable, and confident? Do you think you'd be a better you? Absolutely! Reading 10 pages per day is not going to break you, but it will sure make you.

Final Thoughts on Reading

- Begin with the end in mind—what do you hope to gain from the book? Take a moment to do this now by asking yourself what you want to gain from reading this one.

- Books don't have to be read cover to cover, nor do they have to be finished. Remember that this is your reading time. Be sure to use the table of contents of a book to make sure that you are reading the parts that you care about most, and don't hesitate to put it down and move to another if you aren't enjoying it. There is too much incredible information out there to spend any time on the mediocre.

- Many Miracle Morning practitioners use their reading time to catch up on their religious texts, such as the Bible, Torah, or Quran.

- Feel free to underline, circle, highlight, dog-ear, and take notes in the margins of this book. The process of marking books as you read allows you to come back at any time and recapture all of the key lessons, ideas, and benefits without needing to read the book again. If you read on a digital reader, such as Kindle, Nook, or via iBooks, notes and highlighting are easily organized, so you can see them each time you flip through the book, or you can go directly to a list of your notes and highlights.

- Summarize key ideas, insights, and memorable passages in your journal. You can build your own brief summary of your favorite books so you can revisit the key content any time in just minutes.

- Rereading good personal development books is an underused yet very effective habit. Rarely can you read a book once and internalize all of the value. Achieving mastery in any area requires repetition. I've read books like *Getting Things Done* as many as three times and often refer back to them throughout the year. Why not try it out with this book? Commit to rereading it as soon as you're finished to deepen your learning and give yourself more time to master your Miracle Morning.

- Take advantage of action steps and action plans set out in the books you read. While reading is a great way to learn new strategies, it is the implementation and practice of these new strategies that will improve your life and business. Are you committed to taking action on what you're learning in this book by following through with at least one of the 30-Day Challenges at the end of each chapter?

S is for Scribing

Scribing is simply another word for writing. I write in my journal for five to ten minutes during my Miracle Morning, usually during reading time, and then during an additional period of contemplation. By getting your thoughts out of your head and putting them in writing, you gain valuable insights you'd otherwise never notice.

The Scribing element of your Miracle Morning enables you to document your insights, ideas, breakthroughs, realizations, successes, and lessons learned, as well as any areas of opportunity, personal growth, or improvement. Use your journal to note your writing strengths, what went right in each day's sessions, and add any thoughts you want to remember later and perhaps expand on.

If you're like how Hal used to be, you probably have at least a few half-used and barely touched journals and notebooks. It wasn't until he started his Miracle Morning practice that scribing quickly became a favored habit. As Tony Robbins has said many times, "A life worth living is a life worth recording."

Writing will give you the daily benefits of consciously directing your thoughts, but what's even more powerful are the insights you'll gain from reviewing your journals from cover to cover afterwards, especially at the end of the year.

It is hard to put into words how overwhelmingly constructive the experience of going back and reviewing your journals can be. *The Miracle Morning for Real Estate Agents* co-author, Michael Maher, is an avid practitioner of the Life S.A.V.E.R.S. Part of Michael's morning routine is to write down his appreciations and affirmations in what he calls his Blessings Book. Michael says it best:

"What you appreciate ... APPRECIATES. It was time to take my insatiable appetite for what I wanted and replace it with an insatiable appetite and gratitude for what I do have. Write your appreciations, be grateful and appreciative, and you will have more of those things you crave—better relationships, more material goods, more happiness."

There is strength in writing down what you appreciate and reviewing this material can change your mindset on a challenging day.

There are many worthwhile benefits that come from keeping a daily journal. Here are a few more of my favorites. With daily scribing, you'll:

- Gain Clarity—Journaling will give you more clarity and understanding and allow you to brainstorm, as well as help you work through problems.

- Capture Ideas—You will capture and be able to expand on your ideas, and journaling also prevents you from losing the important ones you are saving for an opportune moment in the future.

- Review Lessons—Journaling provides a place to reference and review all of the lessons you've learned.

Acknowledge Your Progress—It's wonderful to go back and reread your journal entries from a year ago and see how much progress you've made. It's one of the most empowering, confidence-inspiring, and enjoyable experiences. It can't be duplicated any other way.

Effective Journaling

Here are two simple steps to get started with journaling or improve your current journaling process.

1. Choose a Format: Physical or Digital. You'll want to decide up front to go with a traditional, physical journal or a digital journal (such as on your computer or an app for your phone or tablet). If you aren't sure, experiment with both and see which you prefer.

2. Get a Journal. Almost anything can work, but when it comes to a physical journal, there is something to be said for an attractive, durable one that you enjoy looking at. After all, ideally you're going to have it for the rest of your life. I recommend getting a journal that is not only lined, but also dated, with room to write for all 365 days of the year. I've found that having a predesignated (dated) space to write keeps you accountable to follow through each day since you can't help but notice when you miss a day or two.

Here are a few of my favorite physical journals:

- *The Freedom Journal* is a brand new product created by serial entrepreneur John Lee Dumas. It's different from other journals because it uses a goal-setting method format where you focus on your #1 priority and then dedicated the next 100 days to completing it.

- *The Five Minute Journal* (FiveMinuteJournal.com) has become very popular among top performers. It has a very specific format for each day, giving you prompts, such as "I am grateful for ..." and "What would make today great?" It takes five minutes or less and includes an evening option, which allows you to review your day.

- *The Miracle Morning Journal* (available on Amazon or at MiracleMorningJournal.com) is designed specifically to enhance and support your Miracle Morning, keep you organized and accountable, and track your Life S.A.V.E.R.S. each day. You can download a free sample of *The Miracle Morning Journal* today at TMMbook.com to make sure it's right for you.

- BulletJournal.com. The Bullet Journal is a journal you buy or a journal system you incorporate into the journal of your choosing. Either way, it's great!

If you prefer to use a digital journal, there are also many choices available. Here are a few of my favorites:

- The Five Minute Journal (FiveMinuteJournal.com) also offers an iPhone app, which follows the same format as the physical version and also sends you helpful reminders to input your entries each morning and evening. It also allows you to upload photos to create visual memories.

- Day One (DayOneApp.com) is a popular journaling app, and it's perfect if you don't want any structure or any limits on how much you can write. Day One offers a blank page, so if you like to write lengthy journal entries, this may be the app for you.

- Penzu (Penzu.com) is a popular online journal, which you can access from your computer.

Again, the format comes down to your preference and the features you want. Type "online journal" into Google or "journal" into your app store, and you'll get a variety of choices.

Customizing the Life S.A.V.E.R.S.

I want to share a few ideas specifically geared toward customizing the Life S.A.V.E.R.S. based on your schedule and preferences. Your current morning routine might allow you to fit in only a 6-, 20-, or 30-minute Miracle Morning, or you might choose to do a longer version on the weekends.

Here is an example of a fairly common 60-minute Miracle Morning schedule, using the Life S.A.V.E.R.S.

Silence: 10 minutes

Affirmations: 10 minutes

Visualization: 5 minutes

Exercise: 10 minutes

Reading: 20 minutes

Scribing: 5 minutes

You can customize the sequence, too. I prefer to do my exercise first as a way to increase my blood flow and wake myself up. However, you might prefer to do exercise as your last activity in the Life S.A.V.E.R.S. so you're not sweaty during your Miracle Morning. Hal prefers to start with a period of peaceful, purposeful silence so that he can wake up slowly, clear his mind, and focus his energy and intentions. However, this is your Miracle Morning, not mine—feel free to experiment with different sequences and see which you like best.

Final Thoughts on the Life S.A.V.E.R.S.

Everything is difficult before it's easy. Every new experience is uncomfortable before it's comfortable. The more you practice the Life S.A.V.E.R.S., the more natural and normal each of them will feel. Hal's first time meditating was almost his last because his mind raced like a Ferrari and his thoughts bounced around uncontrollably like the silver sphere in a pinball machine. Now he loves meditation, and while he's still no master, he says he's decent at it.

I invite you to begin practicing the Life S.A.V.E.R.S. now so you can become familiar and comfortable with each of them and get a jump-start before you begin The Miracle Morning 30-Day Life Transformation Challenge in chapter 2.

If your biggest concern is still finding time, don't worry; I've got you covered. You can actually do the entire Miracle Morning—receiving the full benefits of all six Life S.A.V.E.R.S. in only six minutes a day! Simply do each of the Life S.A.V.E.R.S. for one minute: close your eyes and enjoy a moment of silence, visualize a single action that you want to mentally practice for the day, say your affirmations (or repeat your favorite affirmation over and over). You can then do jumping jacks, push-ups, or crunches. Then grab a book and read a paragraph and jot down a few thoughts in your journal. These six minutes will serve to set you on the right path for the day—and you can always devote more time later in the day when your schedule permits or the opportunity presents itself.

In the coming chapters, I'll shift gears and talk about the specific strategies you can use to become a prolific writer. Not only will I show how you to overcome those challenges that get in the way of building a consistent writing habit, you will also learn how to make a full-time income *just* from the words you put on paper. So let's head on over to the next chapter to talk about the first step in this process.

— 4 —

Not-So-Obvious Writing Principle #1:

BUILDING THE ROUTINE

"Argue for your limitations, and sure enough they're yours."
—RICHARD BACH, New York Times Best-Selling Author

Imagine the life of a successful writer. Perhaps you picture her sipping a morning coffee on a porch, overlooking a babbling brook, and thinking deep thoughts as she carefully crafts a future bestseller.

The *reality* is a lot messier than this scenario—especially for writers who have only a spare 30 minutes each day.

Writing is often balanced with dozens of other obligations. Like working, cooking, cleaning, exercising, and picking up the kids from school. *Nobody* has the time to dedicate an entire day to *just* this activity.

What's interesting is there is a popular misconception that successful writers have more time than the average person. That the only reason they do well is because they can spend hours each day on their books. That they don't have to worry about pesky chores and errands like everyone else.

The truth is … most successful writers started out just like you. They balanced writing with a full-time job and other responsibilities. Sure, it wasn't easy for them. But they made it happen because they committed to writing, every day, no matter what happened. In other words, they *built a daily writing routine.*

Now, there is no perfect routine. While the Miracle Morning helps you start the day on the right foot, your choice of when to write depends on your schedule and personal situation.

Some people (like myself) prefer to write after their morning routine. Others find their rhythm late at night. And many write whenever they find the time. The only requirement is to *schedule this activity* into your daily routine.

To give you an idea of how routines differ from writer to writer, here are a few routines of popular authors. You'll find that most complete their words in the morning, but there are subtle differences of how they accomplish this daily activity.

The Routines of Famous Writers

Haruki Marakami, who wrote *Norwegian Wood* and *The Wind-Up Bird Chronicle*, dedicates the first part of his day to writing.

He gets up at 4:00 am and writes for five to six hours straight. Then he spends the remainder of the day on activities like running, swimming, reading, and listening to music. The key to his success is repetition and balancing writing with physical activity.

The repetition itself becomes the important thing; it's a form of mesmerism. I mesmerize myself to reach a deeper state of mind. But to hold to such repetition for so long—six months to a year—requires a good amount of mental and physical strength. In that sense, writing a long novel is like survival training. Physical strength is as necessary as artistic sensitivity.

Stephen King is another example of someone who writes first thing in the morning. He believes in a straightforward, almost mechanical, approach to the craft.

Your schedule—in at about the same time every day, out when your thousand words are on paper or disk—exists in order to habituate yourself, to make yourself ready to dream just as you make yourself ready to sleep by going to bed at roughly the same time each night and following the same ritual as you go.

What I love about King's habit is he treats writing like a job. He does it every day, including birthdays and holidays. His goal is to complete 2,000 words, which is usually completed by late morning or the early afternoon.

By comparison, there are authors like **Ray Bradbury**, who wrote whenever and wherever he could. A specific schedule wasn't important. What mattered was that he hit a specific word count on a daily basis.

I can work anywhere. I wrote in bedrooms and living rooms when I was growing up with my parents and my brother in a small house in Los Angeles. I worked on my typewriter in the living room, with the radio and my mother and dad and brother all talking at the same time. Later on, when I wanted to write Fahrenheit 451, I went up to UCLA and found a basement typing room where, if you inserted ten cents into the typewriter, you could buy thirty minutes of typing time.

British novelist and dramatist **R. F. Delderfield** wrote for a specific period of time each day—until 4:00 in the afternoon. Even if he finished a book mid-afternoon, he would stick a new piece of paper in his typewriter and start working on the next book, working until 4:00 pm.

Finally, **Jack Kerouac** wrote later in the day. In an interview (tinyurl.com/kerouacparis) he shared the following:

The desk in the room, near the bed, with a good light, midnight till dawn, a drink when you get tired, preferably at home, but if you have no home, make a home out of your hotel room or motel room or pad: peace.

What's the lesson here? There isn't a *right time* to do your writing. While I recommend the morning because writing pairs nicely with the Miracle Morning (plus it's a time when you'll feel energized), your choice depends on what else you have going on.

Every successful author develops a unique writing practice that suits their needs. Some work best in the early hours of the morning, while other authors write all night and sleep all day. All I suggest is you find a time and stick to it for at least a few weeks. Now, the biggest obstacle to building a routine is knowing how to deal with writer's block. So let's talk about how you can a build a habit that forever eradicates this challenge.

The Reality of Writer's Block

Ever experienced this before?

A great story idea pops in your head. So you do a little bit of research, jot down a few ideas, and then open a document, ready to share it with the rest of the world. Suddenly the words don't come to you. You know it's a great idea, but you're not sure *how* to write it.

Writer's block is a common experience that happens for many reasons. Maybe you're unsure if an idea will work in your market. Or perhaps you're stuck with a certain scene. Or you might simply feel scared that nobody will like your book. It happens to all of us, so it doesn't really matter *why* it occurs. Your job is to know how to overcome writer's block (or even prevent it from happening) by following these four strategies:

1. Separate "Both" Brains into Two Activities

Most writers are perfectionists. As such, we want people to enjoy our content and be entertained, educated, or a combination of both. The problem? It's easy to fall into the trap of tinkering with the copy *as* we're creating the words.

Editing while writing limits you because they are two separate activities that require different skillsets. First, you're creating original thoughts, compelling dialogue, and engaging stories. Second, you're editing these words and tightening the copy. This means that when you try to do both at the same time, your brain is performing two activities that conflict with each other: being creative and ruthlessly chopping unnecessary content.

Now, this isn't just theory. In a 2011 study called the *Neural correlates of creative writing* (tinyurl.com/ncbi-writing), researchers found that planning and organization (which uses the same part of your brain as editing) is completed by one part of the brain while creativity is accessed in another area. In essence, when you try to simultaneously write and edit your brain is attempting to do two different activities.

So the simple solution is to use your creativity while writing the first draft and then leave the editing for the second and third drafts. (I'll talk more about this in Chapter Seven.)

2. Build the Idea-Generation Habit

The worst type of writer's block is when you stare at a blank screen and can't think of what to say next. A quick fix is to create an outline (for nonfiction) or story beats (for fiction) *before* you start writing.

The pre-writing phase is important because these words act as prompts for your narrative. You won't have to worry about a blank screen because you've already mapped out what to say next. And if a great idea pops into your head as you write, you can shift direction and add it to the story.

We'll address the specifics of outlining and story beats later on in *The Miracle Morning for Writers*, but for now let's talk about a few additional strategies for overcoming "blank page syndrome."

The mind is a muscle that should be regularly exercised. One reason you might experience writer's block is that you haven't built the *daily creativity habit*. A solution is to substitute the *Scribing* part of your Life S.A.V.E.R.S. with one of the following activities:

- **Write down your thoughts.** Write about *anything* that comes to mind. The words themselves don't matter or even have to make sense. This is a stream of consciousness exercise where you record all your surface thoughts.

- **Free associate.** Open up the dictionary and pick a word. Jot down everything related to the word that you can think of. It could be a story, a "how-to" article, or a fun memory.

- **Talk about firsts.** Craft a story related to a significant first in your life. This could be a first kiss, first time on an airplane, first time you met your spouse, or first time visiting a favorite travel destination. What really matters here is to connect an idea with a powerful emotion.

- **Write about a picture.** Think of your favorite painting (or simply find an interesting picture on Pinterest or Instagram) then write a story about what happened before or after the picture was taken.

These are just a few exercises that can be incorporated into the morning Life S.A.V.E.R.S. routine. Even 10 minutes a day can have a positive impact on your creativity. While these exercises might seem simplistic, they teach your subconscious to activate your creativity on demand.

3. Stop Comparing Yourself to Famous Authors

The mistake some writers make is they compare themselves to their favorite authors and feel paralyzed because their writing isn't as good. Often they will agonize over spelling, grammar, and everything else in the first draft. Sure, you want to do your best. But it's important to keep in mind that those perfect phrases can happen during the later drafts as well.

For instance, consider that famous opening line from A *Tale of Two Cities* by Charles Dickens:

It was the best of times, it was the worst of times, it was the age of wisdom, it was the age of foolishness, it was the epoch of belief, it was the epoch of incredulity, it was the season of Light, it was the season of Darkness, it was the spring of hope, it was the winter of despair, we had everything before us, we had nothing before us, we were all going direct to Heaven, we were all going direct the other way.

Many consider this to be the perfect opening line, but Dickens probably didn't get it right the first time. Odds are he revised it a number of times, writing and rewriting until it was perfect.

So stop agonizing over the fact that your writing is not as great as your favorite author's. Most of the time, these perfect lines came from years and years of practice. Those genius lines did not come overnight.

4. Avoid and Prevent Distractions

Writer's block is often caused by distractions. You're working on a section and realize you need to research a fact, so you hop on Google, and then you think of something related to social media. Next thing you know, you've spent the last 15 minutes watching cat videos on YouTube.

Scenarios like this often happen when writers don't prepare for distractions. We're creative by nature, so it's easy to go down a rabbit hole whenever we get a great idea. The solution is to create a few rules to prevent and handle any foreseeable interruption.

- Do your research ahead of time while outlining or crafting story beats.

- Jot down a reminder to look up specific facts later during *non*-writing time.

- Time yourself while writing and refuse to respond to any impulse to break your flow. (I'll talk about this more in Chapter Five.)

- Use the full-screen mode if you use the Scrivener (LiteratureandLatte.com) program.

- Quickly record any idea not related to a current book project and then put it into Evernote (Evernote.com) after the writing session is complete.

Writer's block happens to all of us at some point. Fortunately, there are solutions for overcoming it. If you implement these four strategies, you'll find that it's possible not only to overcome it now, but prevent it from happening ever again.

How to Eliminate the "I Don't Feel Like Writing" Attitude

Throughout *The Miracle Morning for Writers*, I show how to make writing part of your daily routine. But none of this advice helps if you're never in the mood to do it.

I get it. Writing is *hard* work. Often, it's hard work on top of the hard work you've had to do for your job. You've had a long day, and the only thing you want to do is plop on the couch and binge watch your favorite series on Netflix.

What's interesting is this is an impulse that all writers have— even the successful ones. We sometimes don't *want* to write, yet we somehow push ourselves to get it done. How is this possible? Well, you can find the answer by diving into a bit of psychology.

Ego Depletion (The Obstacle for Building the Writing Habit)

I want you to take five minutes and do the following exercise.

Write down every task you completed yesterday. Did you work, exercise, do chores, pay bills, or take care of the kids? It doesn't really matter *what* you did; just jot it down so you get a good idea of all that you accomplished in a single day.

Now, imagine writing for 60 minutes *in addition* to these activities. Sounds overwhelming, right? This is a common sensation that happens whenever people try to build *any* new habit. This new routine has to compete with everything else that needs to be done. Your energy levels are low, and the last thing you want to do is write. This is what often happens when *ego depletion* rears its ugly head.

In the book *Willpower*, authors Roy F. Baumeister and John Tierney describe ego depletion as "a person's diminished capacity to regulate their thoughts, feelings, and actions."

Simply put, our willpower is like a muscle. It weakens throughout the day through constant use. Every time you have to make a hard decision ... or resist a temptation ... or focus on a high-level activity, you draw from the same reservoir of willpower.

For instance, think back to those moments when you're unable to resist a tasty treat. It probably happened later in the day *after* you'd completed a dozen tasks and made a series of important decisions. Your mind was tired, and all you wanted was that delicious snack. You caved in because your willpower had diminished and you were unable to resist *another* temptation.

To prove this concept, let's talk about the Radish Experiment, which Baumeister and his colleagues ran. They brought three groups of people into a room and were presented with different options:

- One group was shown chocolate chip cookies and radishes and was told they could eat anything they wanted.

- Another group was offered the same options and was told they could eat only the radishes.

- The final group was brought into a room with no food options.

After that, each group was moved into a separate room where they had to work on a challenging puzzle. The groups that didn't have to exert willpower (those who could eat whatever they wanted or had no food option) worked on the puzzle for an average of twenty minutes. The group that had to exert willpower and resist the tasty treats gave up after eight minutes.

What does this show?

Most people can resist a variety of impulses. However, this effort leaves us in weakened condition where it becomes harder to tap into that pool of willpower.

There are two important lessons here:

1. You have a finite amount of willpower that can become depleted.

2. You use the same stock of willpower for all manner of tasks.

What Baumeister found is that the best time for exerting willpower is first thing in the morning because it slowly drains as the day wears on. Everyone has a limit on this reservoir. Once it's gone, it's hard to focus and resist those temptations.

So while I recommend that you find a time for writing that matches *your* schedule, my best advice is to schedule this activity right *after* your Miracle Morning. That way, even if you have a crazy-busy day, you know that at least you've completed your words.

Now, overcoming ego depletion is just one piece of the puzzle. Another challenge is experiencing a sense of overwhelm when you first get started. Often, it's hard to believe that you have the ability to sit down and crank out a few thousands of words. So let's talk about a simple solution for eliminating this initial resistance.

Mini Habits: A Pain-Free Way to Consistent Writing

Mini Habits is a powerful concept that has revolutionized my writing. This is a term coined by my friend Stephen Guise for a process that's designed to help people overcome their natural impulse to avoid difficult tasks.

The idea here is to prevent people from setting overly-ambitious goals that are impossible to complete on a daily basis. When a person consistently fails with a daily goal, it's easy to lose emotional momentum and then give up.

Stephen's point is it's *not* the habit that causes you to fail. Instead, it's the *expectation* that you place on *how much* or *how long* you will do the habit.

As an example, let's say you set a goal to write 2,000 words on a daily basis. You're able to do it for a few days, but then one day you need to stay late at work, and you go to bed exhausted. You skip the next day of writing because you're simply too tired to crank out 2,000 words.

This pattern continues for the next few weeks when you complete the daily word count on one day but then skip writing on the next day. Finally, you give up on the habit because you simply can't stay consistent with writing 2,000 words a day.

Stinks doesn't it?

Fortunately, you can prevent this from happening by adopting the mini habits strategy. The idea here is to focus on *consistency* instead of a specific goal. Sure, you eventually want to push yourself to hit a certain word count, but it's more important to develop the habit of writing.

The mini habits technique works because it prevents those feelings of overwhelm that happen when you set a goal that is too difficult to do every day. Guise explains it this way:

When people try to change, they usually try to get amped up for the change, but no matter how badly you want the change, you haven't changed yet! As motivation wanes, so does progress. You don't need more motivation: you need a strategy that can leverage the abilities of the current you into a better you.

In other words, the simplest way to create a lasting change is to set a goal that is easy to complete on a consistent basis. So instead of trying to write 2,000 words, your initial goal (for *at least* a few weeks) is to write a paragraph or even a sentence. Obviously, you should *try* to do more, but aim for something that's doable no matter what comes up during the day.

I'll admit a paragraph is a stupidly simple goal, but that's the point here! What you're doing is building that muscle memory to write on a daily basis.

Still not sold on the mini habits concept?

Well, here are five reasons it can help with the development of a writing routine.

1. Your success will lead to more success. It's easy to get discouraged when you fail over and over again. On the other hand, a mini habit will create a sense of excitement because you're hitting an important goal daily. Trust me, when you have a 30-day streak going, it's easier to feel that excitement to get started each day.

2. You will avoid the guilt trip. It's fun to have a streak of consecutive writing days. This is the exact opposite of what happens when you miss day or two. There is nothing to be gained by setting an overly ambitious goal. All this does is create a negative attitude toward an activity that's supposed to be fun.

3. You increase the desire to write. It's easy to procrastinate when you know that every day you have to write *thousands* of words. You'll learn to dread this activity. But by setting an achievable goal, you push past that inertia and get started because the goal seems completely doable.

4. You'll write more than planned. It's easy to feel that mini habits don't apply to "real writers." Perhaps you think a single paragraph isn't enough to achieve your goals. But the interesting thing is that most of the time, once you get started, you convince yourself to keep going and write way more than you'd planned. In essence, you're using the power of self-deception to trick yourself into getting started. Then this creates enough momentum that you'll keep going long after you've passed the daily goal.

5. You'll form a habit. Consistency is more important for building habits than hitting a specific metric. At first, your routine will be triggered by an external cue, like an alarm on your phone. But eventually, you'll simply remember to write at a specific time each day. This is what happens when you build a positive habit into your life. (We'll talk more about cues and why they're important in Chapter Five.)

Throughout *The Miracle Morning for Writers*, I provide strategies for turning writing into a permanent habit, but if you're someone who struggles with getting started, then you can overcome this challenge by creating a mini habit for this activity.

How to Write Daily (Even if You Don't Have the Time)

We all live busy lives, so sometimes it's hard to know exactly *when* you'll have time to write. Not only does ego depletion sap your energy, it's also challenging to carve out that solid block of "me time" that all writers need. That said, thousands of successful authors have experienced these same challenges, yet they still found the time complete their daily words.

For example, Kurt Vonnegut had to teach lessons and grade papers for his job. So he would get up every day at 5:30 a.m. and write until 8:00 a.m. Then he would go to work, enjoy a social life after school, and then call it a day.

Toni Morrison started writing at 4:00 a.m. and continued until her children woke up and she had to get them ready for school.

Fellow self-published author Mark Dawson (SelfPublishingFormula.com) wrote his novels during a daily train commute back and forth to London.

What's the difference between these three writers and the thousands of others who struggle with their consistency?

Each scheduled time for writing and made it happen.

Like you, successful writers have personal obligations, so they find a small pocket of uninterrupted time and make the necessary sacrifices to write on a schedule.

If you feel like there's no time to write, then try one (or all) of these strategies.

1. Write just what you think is enough writing. Think back to the previous section on mini habits. One reason people fail is they set overly ambitious goals. This stems from a common, but dangerous, belief that "real writers" are able to crank out 2,000 words a day.

What most people fail to realize is you can do amazing things through small daily actions. To quote Bill Gates, "Most people overestimate what they can do in one year and underestimate what they can do in ten years."

Think of it this way … Let's say you have only 30 minutes a day to produce an average of 500 words per session.

Doesn't seem like a lot, does it? But, let's do the math and see what happens with consistent butt-in-chair time.

Five hundred words a day is 15,000 words in one month. That's enough for a short nonfiction book. Or if you're a novelist, you can complete a 60,000-word book in four months. Or you would write 182,500 words in one year, which is enough for *three* short novels.

Now, these are the results from *just* 500 words a day. Once you get into a rhythm, it's not hard to consistently write one thousand, two thousand, or even five thousand words daily. There are thousands of writers, right now, who do this *every* day—while working a full-time job. Once you've confidently built the writing habit, you'll discover plenty of opportunities to do a little more writing every day.

2. Barter your time with family and friends. It's almost impossible to write in isolation. Like most folks, you probably have a job, children to support, and relationships to maintain. So it doesn't seem possible to tell the world that you need two hours a day for writing. Instead, talk to your closest allies and make agreements for carving out writing time.

For instance, let's say you need 60 minutes of writing time while your spouse takes care of the kids. In exchange, you could offer 60 minutes where he or she gets to enjoy their favorite activity. You're not *taking* from your relationship. Instead, you're being honest about one of your important needs and looking for a way to support one another.

3. Leverage small pockets of time. Every day, there are numerous opportunities to write—the trick is to know *how* to take advantage of them. Just think of all the small 5 and 10-minute blocks when you're killing time. If you can maximize these moments, then you'll be on your way to a building a consistent habit.

For instance, you could write in these pockets of time:

- While on public transportation, like on a bus or a train
- During your lunch break (and then eat something while answering your work-related email)
- After doing house-related chores at the end of the day

You could also jot down ideas while waiting in line or dictate certain sections using Evernote. (We'll talk more about this app in Chapter Six.)

Finally, you could use free time to knock out those small chores that get in the way of your writing time, like making phone calls, doing online shopping, or completing paperwork.

Your mobile phone gives you the capability to communicate with the world. So I ask you, what's a better use of your time? Spending 10 minutes plotting your next book or playing a few rounds of Candy Crush? By now, I think you know the answer to that question.

Eliminate Limiting Beliefs about Writing

You now know it's possible to find the time for writing and make it happen daily. But what about those moments when you *don't believe* in your ability to create something awesome? That's why it's important to examine your mindset and unlock those limiting beliefs that are holding you back. Here are five that commonly plague writers.

Limiting Belief #1: "Fast writing is bad writing."

Somewhere along the line, our society has created a myth that the best writers spend years working on a book. While there is some benefit to deliberately crafting your book, many successful writers understand the importance of sticking to a tight schedule and producing words at a fast pace.

The truth is you can write fast and still do great work. To illustrate this point, here are a few examples of classic books that were quickly written:

- Jack Kerouac spent seven years traveling and taking notes on his journey, but it took him only a month to write *On the Road*.

- Robert Louse Stevenson completed *The Strange Case of Dr. Jekyll and Mr. Hyde* in two weeks.

- Erle Stanley Gardner, who wrote the popular *Perry Mason* novels, averaged one million words a year.

- Victor Hugo, who wrote *Les Miserables* and *The Hunchback of Notre Dame*, completed 20 pages per day.

- John Grisham, one of the most popular authors around, wrote a novel in 100 days and another in six months.

Remember: You can always delete words you don't like, but you can't do anything with the words that are still stuck in your head.

Limiting Belief #2: "Nobody is interested in what I have to say."

Most of the time, this is a completely invalid excuse. Unless you are covering an esoteric topic like worm farming in Argentina, odds are somebody wants to hear your message.

Remember, the Internet gives you the ability to connect with practically anyone in the world. The world is a pretty big place. This means that somebody, somewhere out there is specifically interested in what you have to say. All you have to do is know how to find readers interested in your content.

Another key point to remember is you can't predict what people will want in the future. I don't think anyone could have anticipated the success of *Fifty Shades of Grey*. But E. L. James wrote the kind of book she liked and then found a market of readers who enjoy her style of erotica.

My advice is to write about topics related to your personal interests because there is a market for it somewhere in the world.

Limiting Belief #3: "I can never figure out what to say."

This is a classic belief related to writer's block. If you learn how to research, plan, and outline (all of which are addressed later in this book), then you won't get stuck. In fact, with the suggestions I provide throughout the *The Miracle Morning for Writers*, you won't ever worry again about what to write. Instead, you can rely on a system where you take that kernel of an idea, flesh it out, and then turn it into content that readers will love.

Limiting Belief #4: "I will never make any money from writing."

There's a saying in the Internet world: "Content is king." Nowadays, all websites and businesses need one thing: words to sell their product or service. This means you can make money through your words with blog posts, freelance articles, self-published books, or even sales copy. If you're a strong enough writer, somebody will pay for your skills.

In Chapter Eight, we'll talk more specifically about how to take your words and generate a reliable income from them. Until then, know that there are tens of thousands of writers who make a full-time income just from their words.

Limiting Belief #5: "My writing isn't good enough."

Many writers don't believe that they can produce quality work. They might struggle with a variety of issues, like spelling, grammar, or syntax. Fortunately, there are many ways to work on your skills while continuously creating content that readers love. The simplest solution is to work with an editor. Not only will this person correct your work, but she will also help you identify common mistakes that you often make.

By working with an editor on a regular basis not only will your skills improve, you will also gain confidence in your skills.

Using Affirmations to Eliminate Limiting Beliefs

These are just five limiting beliefs that might be holding you back. Odds are, you have many other thoughts that run through your head and prevent you from becoming the best writer you can be. So a quick fix is to use affirmations to overcome these limiting beliefs.

In Chapter Three, I talked about Hal's Life S.A.V.E.R.S. method, specifically the "A" (or Affirmations) part of your routine. If you struggle with negative self-talk, then try incorporating the following into your Miracle Morning routine:

- "I can write fast and create content that's worth reading."

- "People love the stories that I'm publishing" (fiction)

- "People get value from what I teach through my writing." (nonfiction)

- "I write best-selling books that readers love."

- "I can overcome a blank page by following my outline or story beats."

- "I always know what to write next. If I can't think of something, then then I will eventually figure it out."

- "My writing is improving every day because I learn from my mistakes and rely on great editors."

- "Writing is a fun activity because it gives me an opportunity to share my thoughts with the world."

- "Writing is profitable, and there are countless ways to make money from this industry."

- "I don't need to depend on an agent or traditional publishing company to make things happen. I can do it on my own by hiring the right people for each aspect of the project."

I'll admit that affirmations might seem a little hokey. However, if your inner voice is full of doubts and negativity, then these statements will help you overcome them and change your thoughts.

Alright, you now understand the psychology behind building a writing routine. You see that it's possible to build the habit, be consistent with it, and actually believe in your ability to follow through with this goal. But perhaps you're not sure *how* to do it on a daily basis.

In the next section, I'll show you how to structure your life so that you can write consistently *without* taking too much of your valuable time. Let's get to it.

Not-So-Obvious Writing Principle #2:

TREAT YOUR WRITING LIKE A JOB

Think back to the routines of the famous writers I mentioned above. Most wrote in the morning, while a few did it either late in the evening or whenever they could find time. The common thread is they all wrote on a *consistent basis*. They had good days or bad days, but no matter what happened in their lives, they completed their words *every* day.

Whenever I think of writing as a consistent habit, I have to mention my favorite example of an author who took a professional approach to his craft. In his autobiography (tinyurl.com/trollopebio), Anthony Trollope discussed how he balanced writing with a day job in the postal service.

Trollope completed almost 50 novels simply by writing in the few morning hours before his day job. In fact, he followed a machine-like schedule that kept him on track. From 5:30 am to 8:30 a.m., with his watch in front of him, Trollope would write 250 words every 15 minutes or 1,000 words per hour. No breaks, 250 words every 15 minutes.

What's even more amazing about Trollope's schedule is his relentless approach to project management. If he completed a novel before the end of a writing session, he wouldn't take the rest of the time off. Instead, he would *immediately* start the next one.

Okay, this schedule might sound a *tad* obsessive, but there is an important lesson to be learned here.

If you take the essence of Trollope's workmanlike approach to writing, you would see it's possible to do great things—even if your days are already overbooked.

The Miracle Morning helps you start the day on the right foot, and you already know it's possible to turn writing into a consistent habit. So let's talk about the nuts and bolts of how to take this passion and transform yourself into a Trollope-like machine that cranks out a consistent number of words—and books.

How to Schedule Time for Writing

A favorite writing quote of mine (often attributed to William Faulkner) is *"I only write when I am inspired. Fortunately I am inspired at 9 o'clock every morning."*

Read that last line a few times until it sinks in.

"Fortunately I am inspired at 9 o'clock every morning."

Faulkner's point was simple. Amateurs wait until they feel motivated before writing. Professionals treat it like a job where they clock in and clock out every day—usually around the same time. They write when motivated. They write when *not* motivated. And sometimes they write when it's the last thing they want to do.

"Fortunately I am inspired at 9 o'clock every morning."

Sure, you might argue that a schedule kills the fun, creative aspect of writing. But the opposite is usually true. By sticking to a schedule, you will train your mind to perform at a specific time and instantly tap into the creative part of your brain. It will be challenging at first, but you will eventually reach a point when you can instantly get to work.

Let me elaborate on this point with an easy example.

At some point, you've probably watched an athletic competition. Most sporting events are scheduled for a standard day and time. Baseball games, basketball games, and football games. Each sport plays around the same time during the season. The athletes don't pick the time. Instead, it's set by the athletic league and team owners.

Can you imagine what would happen if an athlete said, "Gee coach, I'm not feeling motivated to play right now. Could we reschedule the game for later in the day?" He would be laughed at (and probably benched).

Athletes understand they have no control over the game schedule, so they train themselves to achieve peak performance *exactly* when they need to. Those who can't are usually cut.

Fortunately, you can do the same as a writer. By scheduling this activity for a certain time, you'll learn to perform at the exact time you need to.

"Fortunately I am inspired at 9 o'clock every morning."

Now that you know why it's important to schedule time for your writing, let's talk about how to work it into your day. Below I'll cover four factors to consider as you plan out the writing habit.

Consideration #1: How should you write?

I've already talked about the importance of habits. So you shouldn't be surprised that I recommend committing to *at least* five times a week. If your weekends are focused on family time, then it's okay to take off a day. But you should remember that you have to write only for a few minutes to keep that daily consistency.

So, my advice is to set a mini habit goal that's easy to complete no matter what comes up. It could be 10, 20, or 30 minutes a day. Just set a small enough goal that it can fit into any schedule, even on your busiest day.

Consideration #2: When should you write?

The best way to improve your success at writing is to schedule it for a certain time and *never* miss a day (or take only one day off every week). This is how to transition from an amateur to a professional who creates no matter what comes up.

The writing routine I follow is simple: I complete my morning routine and then immediately write for 30 minutes. That's my mini habit goal. Usually, I write for a few hours. But I know that if I'm having a busy day, then it's okay to stop at 30 minutes and do something else.

In addition to setting your small goal, you should also schedule your writing for a specific time. I recommend first thing in the morning.

Here are a few reasons why:

- You won't procrastinate and skip a day if an unforeseen event comes up in the afternoon or evening.

- You are alert and energized first thing in the morning, especially since you just completed your Miracle Morning.

- You will avoid the ego depletion trap where your creative juices are wasted on other activities.

- You will have fewer distractions since the rest of the world is still asleep.

You might have time for only the Miracle Morning in the first part of the day, so you might be forced to schedule writing at a different time. Perhaps you have a busy schedule with obligations like childcare or working, so your first *preference* for when to write might not be possible. The important thing is to find *some* time to write and stick to it!

Once you'ved picked a time of day, block it off on your calendar. This is a sacred time that's as important as any appointment or meeting. It will be 30-60 minutes of time that's dedicated to your writing.

Again, the key point here is to write at a consistent time. This will make it easier to turn it into a consistent habit. Do this for a few weeks, and you'll train your brain to get started right away. You won't suffer from procrastination or other issues; instead you'll learn how to fire up your computer and immediately begin.

Consideration #3: Where should you write?

Does a writing location really matter? I think it does. Where you decide to write has a direct impact on turning it into a permanent habit.

A good location keeps you focused, prevents distractions, makes you feel inspired, and is easily accessed (i.e. within a 10-minute walk or drive). It's a special place that's dedicated to an important routine.

Conversely, a bad place, includes multiple distractions, and is filled with people who ask for just a minute of your time. It's impossible to write there because you can't concentrate for more than a few minutes at a time.

There isn't a right or wrong answer for picking a location. Many writers need absolute silence, while others (myself included) thrive in loud, bustling coffee shops filled with people. What's important is to identify what works for you and go there whenever you need to write. This will condition your mind to get started right away once you're in that familiar space.

Home or Away?

If you decide to write in your home, then you have a few options for setting up a workspace:

- A formal office
- A writing desk tucked away in a secluded corner in your home
- A front porch or back deck
- A section of your dining room table
- A part of your bedroom
- A converted part of your walk-in closet

Really, the only requirement here is to find a space that's free from distractions.

If you can't write from home, then it's possible to do it wherever you can work on a laptop computer. This can include the following:

- Coffee shops
- Diners and dine-in places like Panera Bread
- Office space in a co-working location
- Your local library
- Public places like a park
- Mass transportation like a bus or a train commute

If you choose to write away from home, then be sure to bring certain essentials like your laptop, the outline of your next project, related notes, a pad of paper, many pens, and your preferred writing programs, like Scrivener, Grammarly, or Hemingway. This will turn writing into a mobile habit that can be completed *anytime* and at *any* location.

Consideration #4: How can you create a distraction-free environment?

Picking a location is just a small part of the process. Often, your productivity is affected by your choice in decoration, noise, and level of clutter. That's why it's important to spend a few minutes to set up a space that makes you feel inspired and is free from potential distractions.

To get started, add any (or all) of the following to create a motivational atmosphere:

- Awards, diplomas, or similar items
- Positive reviews from your previous titles
- A list of writing affirmations
- Quotes from successful authors
- A storyboard of your plot or outline of your book
- Pictures of writers who inspire you
- Bookshelves filled with your favorite fiction and nonfiction titles

The amount of stuff you allow in your space depends on your personal preferences. Some like to work in a room filled with items and piles of paper because it makes them feel like a real artist. Others prefer the minimalist approach with only a desk and a computer. I recommend starting with whatever you have in the room and then remove (or move) items that distract you.

How to Minimize Distractions and Interruptions

Distractions are a productivity killer. Even a few minutes could destroy momentum, break your concentration, and make you forget what you wanted to write next.

You also have to consider the cumulative impact of distraction. Sure you might lose only five minutes each day, but add that up over a month (two and half hours) or even a year (more than thirty hours). That's a lot of wasted time! Lost time that has a negative impact on your word count and your revenue as an author.

Remember, the average writer has time for only 30-60-minutes of writing a day. So it's in your best interest to eliminate the distractions that will cut your time and productivity. My suggestion is to take responsibility for preventing interruptions by doing the following:

- Wear earplugs or noise-cancelation earphones.

- Listen to instrumental music or anything that helps you concentrate.

- Invest in a white noise machine (or app), one that comes with sounds like ocean, wind, or rain.

- Work in a space where you can close the door and block out most sounds.

- Sit in a remote part of a park, restaurant, or coffee shop, away from loud talkers or groups.

- Clear your writing desk of all unnecessary items.

- Silence your computer and phone so you won't hear the ding when you get a new email or text message.

- Talk to your roommates, significant other, and children about your writing time. Make it clear that you are not to be disturbed unless there is a true emergency.

- Work offline and disconnect from email, so you won't be tempted to surf the web or get derailed by research.

It's not easy to write on a consistent basis. And distractions only make it more difficult. So the best way to prevent them is to plan ahead and eliminate disruptions from happening in the first place.

Tracking Your Word Count

Writing is a curious activity. Some days the words fly off your fingertips and you create amazing content. Other days, it's a battle to put words together and you wonder why you should even bother with this frustrating activity.

Unfortunately, you can't predict when you'll have a good or bad day. The best thing to do is create a system that identifies your optimal flow state and then engineer your day so writing is completed during these peak moments.

Flow State: A Definition

You've probably had those moments where you feel in the zone. This could be while writing, exercising, or working on a fun project. These are the times when you experience a period of intense motivation and time flies by. This is commonly known as *flow state*.

Flow state was first popularized by Mihály Csíkszentmihályi, who wrote extensively about it in his book *Flow: The Psychology of Optimal Experience*. Csíkszentmihályi makes the point that flow is a state that melds creativity with happiness and occurs when you become deeply immersed in any creative process. This state not only blocks out negative feelings and self-doubt, it also creates a feeling of contentment that lasts after the state ends.

Flow state commonly occurs when you:

- Become 100 percent focused on a task.

- Lose track of what is going on around you. It's difficult to become distracted by the outside world.

- Know exactly what needs to be accomplished and how to do it.

- Lose some of your sense of self and become "one" with the process you are working on.

- Eliminate worries and doubts about your abilities; you forget about your self-limiting beliefs.

- Feel increased happiness and contentment from completing the thing you love.

Put simply, flow state is a magical moment when you experience peak performance and nothing stops you from doing great things.

The downside is that flow state can't be switched on like a light. Some days flow won't come—no matter how hard you try. While you cannot force a state of flow, you can open yourself up to this state of heightened creativity and focus.

Using the lessons learned from Csíkszentmihályi's book, I recommend a simple three-step process that will *increase the likelihood* of achieving peak performance on a consistent basis:

Step 1: Work on Fun Writing Projects

First, the bulk of your writing should focus on genres or niches that you enjoy. Sure, there will be times when you write to pay the bills, but spend most of your days on exciting projects.

To illustrate this point, let me talk about a principle that I teach to students in my *Authority Pub Academy*. I call it the 3Ps:

- Passion—A personal interest, one that you would enjoy talking about even if you weren't writing about it.

- Personal Experience—You have some level of expertise or at least an ability to interview knowledgeable experts and share their experiences.

- Profitability—Something that sells well on eBook platforms like iTunes, Amazon, and Kobo.

I recommend that you write about topics where you have passion and personal experience (if you're writing nonfiction). Profitability is important, but it should be the final consideration after picking a topic that strongly connects to an interest.

With passion, it's easier to come up with good ideas and maintain that long-term interest in this market. Also your subconscious mind will come up with references and anecdotes that will make their way into the copy.

Step 2: Create the perfect flow-state environment

I already covered this in the previous section, but the best way to achieve flow state is remove distractions from your environment. So do these things:

- *Never multitask.* Unless you're listening to soothing background music, doing more than one thing only leads to a cluttered, stressed-out mindset. (According to a recent study out of Stanford {tinyurl.com/stantaskstudy}, people who multitask are less productive than individuals who focus on one task at a time.)

- *Avoid distractions.* Shut the door to prevent people from interrupting you. Turn off email and any app notifications. Every distraction could prevent a state of flow. So be mindful about these interruptions and look for ways to prevent them from happening.

- *Focus on the moment.* Your attention should be on the current project and nothing else. Try to empty your mind of thoughts like bills, other projects, or what you saw on television last night. Just think about what you are working on currently.

I've already talked about preventing distractions in this chapter, so I won't list the steps again. The important thing to remember is that your flow state is a fragile thing, so do everything you can to make sure you won't get interrupted.

Step 3: Work in time blocks

Good writers use time to their advantage by knowing how to ignore distractions while they're on the clock. If you're someone who has trouble focusing, then try condensing your writing into short sprints and track them with a timer. A system for doing this is called the *Pomodoro Technique.*

The *Pomodoro Technique* (pomodorotechnique.com) is a popular time blocking system created in the 1980s by Francesco Cirillo that has been embraced by entrepreneurs and work efficiency experts.

Cirillo recognized that humans can focus only for a limited amount of time before becoming distracted. He found that it's better to create a system where people focus for a condensed period of time and then proactively take a rest break before beginning the next sprint.

Cirillo named his technique after a popular kitchen timer that looks like a tomato (hence the name pomodoro, which is Italian for tomato). The timer was used like any old kitchen timer, but Cirillo experimented with time blocking until he discovered the most effective usage of time blocks (for efficiency in work production).

When using the technique, you:

1. Choose a task (e.g., writing).

2. Set a timer for 25 minutes.

3. Work for 25 minutes without succumbing to any distractions.

4. Take a five-minute break by getting up and walking around.

5. Go back to work for another 25 minutes.

6. After every four time blocks take a 15–30 minute break.

So to put it all together, if you set aside 120 minutes for writing with the Pomorodo Technique every day, you would write for a total of 100 minutes, with three, five-minute breaks between the sessions.

You might assume that this technique is not as effective as writing without breaks. But think back to those times when you tried to do a task for an extended period of time. In all likelihood, you were energized at first, and then you reached a point when your concentration dropped off, and finally you felt the urge to do anything *besides* writing.

The Pomodoro Technique prevents these distractions because it keeps your mind fresh and focused. With the scheduled rest breaks, you have an opportunity to take a few minutes off to relax. So even though you're writing for less time, the quality of the content will be better than what's normally created at the tail end of a marathon writing session.

If you're interested in the Pomodoro Technique, you might want to download one of the following programs to start tracking your words.

- Team Viz (a program that syncs between your computer and mobile phone.) (pomodoroapp.com)
- Rapid Rabbit (iPhone and iPad apps) (rapidrabbit.de/pomodoro)
- Flowkeeper (PC users) (tinyurl.com/gqo867c)
- Pomodoro (Mac users) (pomodoro.ugolandini.com)
- Pomodoro (Android users) (tinyurl.com/pomodroid)

When it comes to time blocking, the amount of time you choose really depends on your personal preference.

I like the Pomodoro Technique because it has a nice symmetry. The 25 minutes on and 5 minutes off is 30 minutes. Four of these fit into two hours, which I consider to be a good day of writing.

Some people prefer short, five- or eight-minute sprints, while others like to write for a solid hour without a break. My advice is to play around with different amounts until you find a routine where you frequently write in an energized, flow state without feeling distracted.

The Importance of Tracking Your Writing Habit

It's important to recognize the flow states when you feel like you could write forever and which elements best support that state for you. A simple way to do this is to track your writing and use this information to identify those moments of heightened productivity. To get started, open a spreadsheet and create nine columns with the following labels:

- Date
- Time of day (morning, afternoon, or evening)
- Location (office, coffeehouse, train)
- Project name (What are you writing?)
- Type of writing (outline, first draft, or second draft)
- Total time blocks for the session
- Total word count
- Average word count per block (divide word count by the number of time blocks)
- Notes of anything that helped or hindered your writing

Update this tracking sheet immediately after completing a session. At first, this might seem like needless busywork. But do it for a few weeks, and you'll detect patterns in your word counts and when you work best.

You'll identify a specific time of day and location where you do your best work. This is the best way to achieve your optimal flow state. Then all you have to do is write in that location at a specific time.

For instance, after using the tracking sheet for a few weeks, I identified two of my personal flow states: The first happened at the start of the day *after* my morning routine. The second was in the early afternoon at a local Starbucks. Now all I have to do is engineer my day to write during these peak moments.

The tracking habit shows when and where you work best. Simply take five minutes every day to record this data and discover your flow state moments, and this will have a positive impact on your writing.

How to Create Your Tracking Form

If you're interested in a print-ready template of the tracking sheet I use, then be sure to check out our resources section. You have two options here:

1. Use an Excel-compatible program where you can modify the document on a computer.

2. Print out the PDF version and manually jot down your daily word count.

If you want to create your own tracking form, then simply open any spreadsheet program and create nine-columns using the information mentioned above.

Be as accurate as possible when first getting started. Diligently record your word counts and add any thoughts in the Notes column about the distractions that pop up. Some common reasons include:

- You were busy and didn't have enough energy to write for very long.

- You procrastinated on writing until the end of the day (and then forgot to do it).

- You allowed friends, co-workers, or family members to interrupt you.

- You were distracted by email or Facebook.

- You researched an idea and went down the Google rabbit hole.

Don't be afraid to be brutally honest. Not only will it help you prevent these distractions from coming up again, you will also gain clarity on what a good day of writing really looks like.

The last thing I want to say about flow state is that consistency is more important than a high word count. It's better to write a little bit each day instead of taking the feast or famine approach where you can't reliably sit down and write for a specific period of time. That's why it's important to *never break the chain*.

A Lesson on NOT Breaking the Chain

One of the most interesting habit-related stories I've ever heard comes from the popular comedian Jerry Seinfeld. When talking to a budding comedian, Seinfeld gave a simple piece of advice (tinyurl.com/seinfeldadvice): set aside time every day to create new material. The key here is to never miss a day, even if you're not in the mood. (Sounds like familiar advice, right?)

At the start of every year, Seinfeld hangs a one-year calendar on his wall and makes a big, red X on the calendar for every day he writes new comedy material. He doesn't have to write a lot of material every day. What's important is to do something every single day, without fail. His focus is to *never break the chain*.

Marking X's on a calendar encourages you to complete your desired task every single day. The more you look at an unbroken string of red Xs, the more compulsion you'll feel to get over any initial resistance and force yourself to get started.

Many great authors follow a similar system in their writing, even if they don't use a calendar with big red Xs. Stephen King, Ernest Hemingway, Kurt Vonnegut, and Isaac Asimov all write (or wrote) something every single day.

The purpose of not breaking the chain is to eliminate your excuses. Often writers think of creative reasons not to get started. We're creative people by nature, and it's easy to turn that creativity to something negative, where you come up with a variety of excuses for *why* you can't write.

My advice is simple: Create a doable daily goal that can be achieved no matter what happens, and don't let yourself be talked out of it. Perhaps you'll set a mini habits goal where you write at least a paragraph a day. Or maybe you'll pick a modest goal of 30 minutes of writing a day. The choice is really up to you. All I ask is that you set a goal that can be achieved even if you have an off day.

Two Ways to Increase Word Count

I've already talked about the importance of consistency and why it's important to write five to seven times a week. But what can you do if you've *already* created the writing habit and *still* can't hit a high word count?

You have two options here: Either you increase your typing speed *or* you dictate your writing. In this section, I'll briefly talk about each option and how it can become your secret weapon to getting more done in the same amount of time.

Option #1: Increase Your Typing Speed

Mastering your typing is the low-hanging fruit of increasing word count. The reality is that many people still use the hunt-and-peck method instead of touch-typing, which is the fastest method for writing.

If you use two fingers to write, then you should learn how to touch-type. Look at the numbers to see why it's important to make this transition:

- Typical hunt-and-peck typists produce 25 words per minute.
- Touch typists can produce, on average, 40 words per minute.
- Good touch typists produce over 60 words per minute.

Another benefit is you will make fewer mistakes. Not only do typing errors reduce your typing speed, they also ruin your train of thought and derail productivity. When you learn how to type with limited mistakes, you consistently produce a high word count.

Enroll in a Typing Class?

I get it. The idea of enrolling in a typing class sounds horrible. For me, it brings up a memory of repeatedly typing, "The quick brown fox jumps over the lazy dog." Fortunately, you can improve your typing speed by following a simple three-step process.

First, record your typing speed. You can use a simple tool like Typing Test (TypingTest.com), which only takes 60 seconds to complete. If you want the test to be completely accurate, then re-take it a few times and average the results.

Next, see where you rate on the typing scale. Ten to 25 words per minute is slow, 26 to 45 is average, 46 to 60 is fluent, 61 to 80 is fast, and 81 and above is pro. If you rate anything less than fluent, then take the next step to improve your typing speed.

Finally, download a software program that teaches touch typing. There are dozens of good options. But, my favorite (and how I learned this skill) is the *Mavis Beacon Teaches Typing* program (developinggoodhabits.com/mavis), which has been around for almost 30 years.

If improving your word count is an important goal, then you should take the time to learn touch-typing. Sure, this might eat into your writing time for a few weeks, but it's a worthwhile investment because your future book projects will be completed faster than before.

Option #2: Dictate Your Writing

Dictation is the best way to create fast outlines and first drafts. The idea is simple. You download a software program, put on a headset, and then narrate the content. It's a great way to quickly get through your first drafts.

Unless you are a fast typist, dictating the first draft can increase your word count by 100 to 200 percent. Remember people speak much faster than they can write. So it's possible to create multiple *thousands* of words per hour. Some authors have even reported that this technique has increased their writing speed to 5,000 words per hour.

Now, I won't lie to you. At first, the drafts produced by narration won't be great because it takes time to familiarize yourself with the dictation software. Keep in mind that you're not trying to create perfect prose. Your goal is to get your thoughts in order and recorded. So you will need to go back over the copy and heavily edit it.

Dictation is also ergonomic. Instead of taxing your hands on a daily basis (and causing issues like carpal tunnel syndrome or arthritis), the speech-to-text option can either alleviate a lot of pain or prevent it from ever happening.

The final benefit is that dictation breaks the editing-while-writing habit. As I've discussed, editing and writing are two separate activities. With dictation, you can't go back and correct any mistakes. So you'll quickly learn to get through a draft without feeling the urge to go back and change things. Ultimately, this will teach you to trust in the process of writing fast first drafts and then clean things up in the second and third drafts.

How to Dictate Your Writing

Great dictation starts with great equipment. I recommend *Dragon Naturally Speaking* (Nuance.com/dragon), which is widely considered to be the best voice-to-text program on the market. This program is not usable right out of the box because you need to "train" it to adapt to your voice and style of dictation. Sure, this takes a bit of time, but it's an investment that will help you consistently write thousands of words per hour.

Another piece of equipment you'll need is a quality, but not expensive, microphone. This is an area where it's easy to overspend on devices with dozens of features. My advice is to stick with something simple like the Logitech Headset H390, which costs around $20 to $30.

More on Dictation

There is a lot more involved with dictating a book. I've done it only in a limited capacity, so if you're interested, you should check out the following two books which will walk you through the entire process:

- *5,000 Words per Hour* by Chris Fox
- *Dictate Your Book: How To Write Your Book Faster, Better, and Smarter* by Monica Leonelle

Both books provide a good starting point for learning about dictation. They tell you what tools you'll need and show you how to get started—*without* feeling that frustration writers often experience with this new technology.

6 Tools to Improve Your Writing Skills

There are a handful of tools that can help you refine your craft, store book ideas, and turn writing into a profitable activity. In this section, I'll go over six applications that will save you a lot of the headaches related writing.

1. Scrivener (LiteratureAndLatte.com): This is an indispensable writing tool that many authors love. With Scrivener you can:

- Organize all your notes, outlines, and drafts in a single location.

- Set word count targets for both your writing session and the entire project.

- Block out distractions by writing on a screen that takes up your entire computer.

- Reorder and organize sections without a lot of hassle.

- Use split screens where you have research open right next to your writing.

- Format the finished product in a variety of file types, which makes it easy to self-publish on the various platforms.

If you want to turn writing into a full-time activity, then Scrivener is a low-cost tool (around $40 to $50) that can manage the entire process.

2. Evernote (Evernote.com): I'll cover Evernote more extensively in Chapter Six, so I won't get into the weeds here except to say that this it's the perfect tool for organizing your research—even if you're a loyal Scrivener user.

The primary benefit of Evernote is it syncs with every type of device. So if you see (or hear) a great book-related idea, you can quickly enter it into the application, put it into a book-specific folder, and then add it to your manuscript during the next writing session.

Moreover, Evernote supports all types of media, so you can add written notes, video, audio, and documents to the app. This gives you a lot of flexibility when it comes to researching your next book.

3. Team Viz (PomodoroApp.com): As I've discussed, the Pomodoro Technique is a time management strategy preferred by many writers. It's not always easy to keep track of the non-writing tasks related to each project. With the Team Viz app, you can transform your writing into a series of bite-sized Pomodoros and keep track of each session.

This software combines the Pomodoro Technique with the method discussed in David Allen's *Getting Things Done* (GTD). GTD teaches you to take *any* massive project and turn it into a series of actionable tasks. Through Team Viz, you can create a new project for your next book, identify all the required steps, and then set deadlines for important milestones.

4. Grammarly (Grammarly.com): This proofreading application is an improved version of your standard spellchecking program. Simply copy and paste blocks of text into Grammarly, and it will check your writing for common mistakes. The reason it's better than most spellcheckers is that it provides useful feedback that will improve the overall quality of your writing.

With Grammarly you get:

- A spell checker that's better than Word or similar programs
- Useful explanations for grammar mistakes (e.g., writing in the passive voice)
- A check for improper word usage
- Context optimized synonyms
- A plagiarism checker with citation suggestions

Of course, Grammarly is no substitute for hiring a professional editor. However, you can use it as a bridge between *your* final version and what's sent to an editor. That way, you get that initial feedback on how to improve your writing, and your editor can focus on the big picture aspects of your project.

5. Hemingway Editor (HemmingwayApp.com): Great writing is simple writing. It doesn't matter if it's fiction or nonfiction, your narrative should get to the point and keep the language simple. With the Hemingway software, you will learn how to simplify your writing.

Hemingway works similarly to Grammarly. You copy and paste text, and the program highlights specific items to edit. It uses a color-coded system where it points to certain areas to improve like:

- Instances of complex words or phrases
- Long, run-on sentences
- Overuse of adverbs

Hemingway also provides the reading level of your work. It might seem counterintuitive, but readability is more important than using fancy words. So the application recommends that you aim for a fifth grade reading level. This will make it simple for anyone to understand your narrative.

6. Cloud Based Storage: These services provide a central location where you can store all your writing, which protects it from a hack or the total loss of your computer. Sure, you can do can store a writing project in Scrivener, but it's a smart move to store your files in a cloud-based service because you'll be doubly-protected from any catastrophic event.

There are many options when it comes cloud-based storage. Here are four of the best options:

- DropBox
- Google Drive
- Box
- Amazon Cloud

Each of the above is a good starting point for managing files. I prefer DropBox since most people use it and I can share folders with the key people in my life. However, the other three are also great options. You can check out each one and then pick the service that is the perfect combination of cost and ease of use.

You now know how to build the writing habit, find time for this routine, and take a professional approach to your craft. Now it's time to dive into the process for thinking of great ideas and never losing out on important thoughts. In the next chapter, I will go over a few simple strategies for keeping track of all those brilliant thoughts that run through your head every day.

— 6 —

NOT-SO-OBVIOUS WRITING PRINCIPLE #3:

TRACKING YOUR BRILLIANT IDEAS

"Million dollar ideas are a dime a dozen. The determination to see the idea through is what's priceless."
—Robert Dieffenbach

We all have great ideas. They often come out of nowhere—popping into your mind at the weirdest moments. Like when you're exercising, showering, doing chores, and talking to others. These thoughts might relate to a new book idea. Or it could be a new strategy for your book-based business. It doesn't matter *when* or *where* you get an idea. What's important is to capture it!

Have you ever had a great thought that you didn't write down? What usually happens? Odds are, you've forgotten it an hour later. Then you're frustrated because you *know* it was a great thought, but you just can't remember it.

The solution to this problem is simple: develop the idea capture habit where you either jot down your thoughts in a journal or record them in an application like Evernote.

When you add this strategy to your daily routine, you'll *never* feel stuck about what to write next. That's because you're consistently adding to your "content idea garden" and giving your subconscious mind an opportunity to think of great writing projects.

The Benefit of the Idea Capture Habit

You might think it's corny to track your ideas, but you would be amazed at the usefulness of this habit—even when you don't take action on a specific thought.

For instance, when you jot down a thought, you'll think of a second (or even a third and fourth) idea related to the first one. What happens next is you'll do an impromptu brainstorming session where you might map out an entire book or piece of content.

Sure, 9 times out of 10, the idea won't go anywhere. But I guarantee you have *at least* one million-dollar idea rolling around in your noggin. All you have to do is get it out of your head and put it somewhere where you can follow up on it.

Two Examples of Million-Dollar Ideas

We've all heard the expression million-dollar idea, which is simply a way of expressing how a single thought can led to a revolutionary business model or piece of technology.

Bill Gates had a simple idea to put a computer in every home.

Ray Kroc wanted to take the McDonald brothers hamburger system and franchise this restaurant all over the United States.

Elon Musk's goal is to make electric cars part of a future that focuses on renewable energy.

These are three famous examples of million (or actually billion) dollar ideas. So let me talk about two people you're hopefully familiar with—Hal and Steve (the authors of this book if you haven't been paying attention).

Hal used the simple concept of the Miracle Morning practice to recover after his accident. Not only did it improve his life, but he quickly realized it could also help others. So he wrote a book sharing the Miracle Morning concept with the world. When this book took off, he turned it into a brand that includes live events, training courses, and a thriving Facebook community. Heck, he's even taken the Miracle Morning framework and is working with authors who specialize in other areas to incorporate their thoughts into the concept. (Which is why you're reading this book.)

I've also had the occasional million-dollar idea. For instance, there was one simple thought came to mind while on vacation in August 2012:

What if I took my blog content and turned them into short, actionable Kindle books?

It was a simple thought—like many others—but the difference was I wrote it down, turned it into a project list, and then immediately took action after my vacation. It was *this* thought that led to earning *almost* a million dollars from my self-publishing business. (I'm hoping to reach this mark by the middle of 2016.)

You never know when you'll have a million-dollar idea. So my suggestion is to write down every thought that occurs to you. Then review each one on a regular basis to see if it's worth pursuing.

Reading = Million-Dollar Thoughts

Garbage in, garbage out.

This is a popular computer science expression that has made its way into the personal development field. If you enter bad programming, you'll get an equally bad outcome. That's why it's important to feed your mind with quality information daily. Only then is it possible to come up with great book ideas.

You might not have considered that your reading and entertainment choices have a direct impact on your success as a writer. If your days are spent looking at the *33 Epic Selfie Fails* on Buzzfeed or *Keeping up with the Kardashians*, then you're limiting your ability to write something great. Garbage in, garbage out.

It doesn't matter if you're a fiction or a nonfiction writer—reading quality books is a good habit to build.

Stephen King said it best: "If you don't have time to read, you don't have the time (or the tools) to write. Simple as that."

Of course, we're all starved for time, so I understand why you might not have hours to kick back with a great book. Fortunately, Hal provides a shortcut with the "R" part of the Life S.A.V.E.R.S. practice. All you have to do is spend 10 minutes a day reading something inspirational.

That said, since reading has a positive impact on your writing, I urge you to take it a step further. My recommendation is to set aside additional time at the end of the day (perhaps before bed) to do any of the following:

- Read books about writing. The market is full of actionable guides that help you improve your grammar, map out stories, come up writing prompts, and learn how to structure a story.

- Read books about entrepreneurialism, personal development, building businesses, and successful people. Not only are these inspiring, but they can also teach you how to transform your writing into a full-time income.

- Spend five minutes each day reading something outside of your personal interests. If you're a staunch Republican, then go to a pro-Democrat website and read an article—with an open mind. This will help you look at the world through a different lens.

- Read books *in* your genre to get an idea of how other authors tell a story, use characters to engage the plotline, and what tropes are commonly used.

- Read books *outside* of your genre. Perhaps you can take an idea that worked in one genre and use it somewhere else. For example, there are many who say *House of Cards* is like a modern day version of *Game of Thrones*.

Challenge yourself to read all of the top 100 classic books (tinyurl.com/h2ot9jv) by the time you die.

I can't overemphasize the importance of reading. Not only does it lead to million-dollar thoughts, it also cultivates a curiosity about the world. Think of reading as an investment that you make in yourself. The more you do it, the more you'll grow as a person.

How to Get Inspiration from the Outside World

Reading books is just one way to upload great thoughts into your mind. I also recommend that you increase the amount of *external* stimulation in your life.

I've talked about achieving the flow state while writing. What's interesting is you can get the same result while doing the activities that don't require a lot of brain power (like driving or doing chores). It's during these times that great ideas often come to mind.

So do the following and pay close attention to the thoughts filtering through your mind:

- Exercise on a regular basis.
- Have a non-writing related hobby, like painting, gardening or doing puzzles.
- Expand your social life and meet new people.
- Pay close attention to advertisements and other promotions that you see throughout the day.
- Turn your driving time into an educational opportunity by listening to audiobooks and podcasts.
- Visit local venues like museums, parks, neighborhoods, graveyards, and historical landmarks.
- Watch a great TED talk.
- Go to a local bookstore to browse books and magazines.
- People watch at a local mall or outdoor shopping plaza.
- Look at Tweets, Pinterest pins, and Facebook updates to see which topics are trending and to identify the content that best resonates with your contacts.

We live in an age of information overwhelm, so you should selectively filter out most of the noise in the world. But, when you set aside time each week to feed your mind with outside perspectives you'll consistently come up with great ideas for the next writing project.

Where to Capture Your Ideas

Where you choose to capture your ideas depends on your preference. While I have my personal favorite (Evernote), I also recognize that everyone has different creative processes. So if you're interested in jotting down those great thoughts, then let me suggest five different options:

1. A pocket-sized notebook. Just think of those old cop shows on television. A detective carries around a small notebook in his coat pocket for interviewing witnesses and jotting down important information. You can do the same thing by carrying a small pad, like the 3.5 by 5.5 inch notebook by Moleskine (tinyurl.com/pocketskine).

2. The Miracle Morning Journal (tinyurl.com/tmmjournal). This product is the perfect companion piece to anyone interested in building the Miracle Morning habit. The benefit of this journal is it helps you clarify goals and projects. Not only can you track the success of your Life S.A.V.E.R.S., you also have a place to record those big ideas.

3. The Freedom Journal (thefreedomjournal.com). This is a product recently launched by John Lee Dumas, a popular entrepreneur and podcaster. The Freedom Journal is a powerful tool for focusing on a single major goal and working on it for the next 100 days. If you have an important book project, then this is a great journal for tracking your progress.

4. Notes Apps. Your mobile phone is a useful tool for storing information. If you're looking for a simple tool, then the Notes app is a decent option. It's not sophisticated, but it works in a pinch when you absolutely have to record an idea and put it *somewhere*.

5. Evernote. In my opinion, Evernote is the best place to store your ideas. Not only can you organize your thoughts, it also syncs with all of your devices. So you could record an idea in Evernote while walking and then access it during your next writing session.

I've given you five great options for recording those million-dollar thoughts. But as I mentioned before, the top solution for organizing these thoughts is Evernote. So let's talk about this app and how it can revolutionize your writing routine.

Using Evernote to Organize Ideas

Let start by answering a basic question: What is Evernote?

Evernote is a cross-platform tool that allows you to take notes, capture ideas, and organize this information into a file structure that's based on your personal needs.

What separates Evernote from other note-taking apps is its flexibility. For the beginner, the app allows you to add notes and easily keep track of them. But there are a number of advanced features that can be used to manage every aspect of your digital life.

Evernote allows you to create simple, text-based notes. But you can also upload photos, record voice reminders, add videos, and clip specific webpages. Anything that can be digitized can be uploaded to Evernote.

To illustrate this point, imagine you're writing a book that takes place during the Mardi Gras season in New Orleans. Naturally, you'd take a trip to this city (only for "research purposes," of course). With Evernote, you could create a variety of book-specific notes.

You could record a video of the Bacchus floats, clip a recipe of King Cake, take pictures of Marie Laveau's vault (and other gravesites in the Saint Louis Cemetery), and record a second line parade. All of these items can quickly be captured, stored digitally in the cloud, and played back as a multimedia experience while working on your book.

Hopefully this demonstrates what's possible with Evernote. It's a flexible app filled with hundreds of options, so it's easy to feel overwhelmed by all the possibilities. One simple solution is to map out a smart file structure and stick to it, which is what I'll talk about next.

The Evernote File Structure for Writers

At its core, Evernote uses a *very* simple file structure. In fact, there are only three ways to organize information with this tool: notes, notebooks, and stacks. You can also find The Miracle Morning resources here: www.MiracleMorning.com/start-here/

Notes are the individual items or files that you upload to Evernote.

- Documents
- Personal notes
- Web page snippets
- Links to Web pages
- Images
- PDF Files
- Videos
- Audio recordings

My advice is to upload one piece of content for each note. That way, you can easily locate any specific item—no matter how many you've already added.

Notebooks are used to categorize your notes. I suggest that you organize them based on specific projects. So whenever you begin a project, create a new notebook. For instance, if you write books, then there should be a separate notebook for each of these books.

Stacks are collections of notebooks. A stack represents a major area of your life, so you might have one for each of the following:

- Writing projects
- Health and exercise
- Finances
- Relationships
- Hobbies

Ideally, you would want to create a stack *only* for the major areas of your life. So if you don't take notes for your hobbies, then it's okay not to include it on the list. The important thing is to create an organizational system that works for you.

Seven Steps for Building Your Evernote System

You probably have dozens of great thoughts every day, and as I've discussed, you need to put them in a central location. That's why I recommend a seven-step process for using Evernote to organize these thoughts.

Step 1: Install Evernote on your mobile phone. This app can best serve you when it's available at *all* times. So take a few minutes *right now* to install it on your phone and create a free account.

Step 2: Create a notebook for each book idea. Get into the routine of creating a notebook the moment you think of a book idea, even if you're not sure if it's something you'll actually write. This is the best way to build consistency with writing down your ideas.

Step 3: Create notes whenever you get an idea. This goes back to what I said about cultivating curiosity about the outside world. Whenever you see something that's inspiring, create a note for it. You can write down the idea, take a photo, or simply dictate the thought, all of which can be recorded in Evernote.

Step 4. Install Web Clipper on your desktop or laptop computer. Evernote's Web Clipper (evernote.com/webclipper) tool can be used to capture articles, links, images, and other types of online content. It's similar to your browser's bookmarking feature, but it's a little different because you can grab snippets of content and store only these sections instead of the entire page.

Web Clipper is great for writers who do a lot of computer-based research. Whenever you come across something interesting, simply clip and add it to a notebook related to your writing project.

Step 5: Group writing notebooks together in a stack. Evernote lets you create a stack by grouping two or more notebooks together. So if you have multiple writing projects, then you want to keep things simple and put them all into a single stack. That way, you have central location for *all* of your writing.

Step 6: Use IFTTT.com to automate your Evernote activities. IFTTT is the acronym for *If This Then That*. The purpose of this site is to coordinate different applications and create a series of automated rules. With a smart combination of recipes, you can streamline the repetitive activities that need to be completed on a regular basis.

For instance, let's say you use Gmail as your email provider. With IFTTT, you can create a simple recipe or process to automatically send certain emails to the Evernote app. This might save only a few seconds per message, but if you create a whole series of automated rules, you can save a serious amount of time that can be invested in your writing.

To learn more, check out the Evernote page on IFTTT (IFTTT.com/Evernote).

Step 7: Review Evernote on a weekly basis. Ideas are nothing without action. Throughout the week you'll add thoughts to Evernote, but this effort will be wasted *unless* you review these ideas regularly.

You complete two activities during this session:

First, transfer the research to the appropriate notebook. Throughout the week, you'll probably have added dozens of notes. Some will end up in the right section, while others might be misplaced. So you should go through all your new notes and make sure they're filed in the right spot. After that, identify and schedule the tasks required to take immediate action on what you've recorded.

Second, start planning your next book. The simplest way to increase your writing productivity is to always have something to work on. Even if you're already in the middle of a project, you can use this time to flesh out ideas for the next one.

The weekly review doesn't have to be a marathon session. All you have to do is identify current projects, go through your notes, and schedule important tasks for the following seven days.

Evernote is a great app for writers. Not only does it organize ideas, it also helps you make smart decisions about what to work on next. Most importantly, Evernote provides a central place to upload all your research.

If you're unclear about *how* to research a writing project, then pay close attention to the process detailed in the next section.

How to Research Your Writing Project

Great writing comes from solid research. So you should set aside time, before writing a word, to plan out the facts that will be included in the narrative.

How much research depends on the specific writing project. If you're writing a fantasy novel, then it might be challenging to interview dragons and wizards. But if you're writing a police procedural novel, then take the time to talk to an authority and make sure to get your facts straight.

Fortunately, we live in an amazing time where most research can be done from the comfort of your home. So here are seven ways to research your next writing project:

Idea #1: Interview knowledge experts. Details are important whether you're writing a piece of fiction or nonfiction. So if your story features an ex-Navy Seal who gets into frequent firefights, then talk to a gun aficionado and understand the weapons they commonly use.

Don't just look up facts on the Internet. Send an email (or even better, pick up the phone) and talk to someone who can provide solid facts. Introduce yourself, say you're writing a book, and ask for just 10 minutes of their time to ask a few questions. You'd be surprised at how often people *love* to talk about their area of interest.

There are plenty of ways to find authorities for any topic. You could leverage your existing social network to see if someone knows a person you could interview. You could also Google the topic and look for authorities. Finally, there are a few websites that can help you track down authorities on any topic:

- LinkedIn (Linkedin.com) is the largest social network for professionals. Enter a phrase in the search bar, and you'll discover thousands of folks who have a background in the subject matter. For instance, if you search under "people" for ballistics you'll discover over 7,000 experts on this topic.

Now, I *wouldn't* recommend contacting strangers and then sending dozens of questions. Instead, introduce yourself, explain *why* you're connecting, and ask if they can talk for a few minutes. If someone charges for their time, then offer to pay their current rate.

- Help a Reporter Out (HARO) (helpareporter.com) is widely used by journalists to find quotable sources. HARO is also available to the general public, so you can create a project and solicit opinions from top authorities in this industry. Simply describe what you're writing and schedule an interview to get more information.

- Just Answer (justanswer.com) can be used to find experts who will answer specific questions for a fee. Here you can talk to lawyers, doctors, mechanics, home improvement experts, and even authorities on firearms.

- Quora (Quora.com) is a platform where you can ask questions and receive answers from people who actually know the topic. Quora is free, so the quality of the answers depends on who responds, but the site has grown enough in popularity that it attracts legitimate experts for most subjects. If you can't find an answer from the other three options, then Quora works well in a pinch.

Idea #2: Visit locations (or rely on places where you've lived). The setting of a good story is as important as a well-written character. It sets the mood for the entire narrative. The simplest way to craft a compelling setting is to visit the location, rely on a memory of a place you've visited, or talk to someone who lives or has visited the place.

For instance, one of the most interesting places I've ever visited is the Sedlec Ossuary in the Czech Republic. Sounds pretty innocent, right? Well, this small chapel contains the skeletons of thousands of people, all arranged in an assortment of decorations (for instance, a chandelier made out of bones). If I ever decide to write a horror story set in Eastern Europe, then you better believe I'll include a scene here.

Idea #3: Use Google Maps. Maybe you don't have the funds to travel or you need to hit a tight deadline. The next best thing is to use the "Street View" feature in Google Maps. This is a quick tool to get an accurate feel for a setting without having to travel there yourself. With Google Maps, you can do a virtual walk-through of an area and check out its surroundings.

Idea #4: Go to a library. Yes, most information can be found on the Internet, but often the best place to do research is at a local library (or one in the nearest city).

Libraries are useful when you need to find information but don't know where to look. You can trigger your creative brain by browsing through books, looking at old photos of the region, reading old newspapers, and scrolling through journals related to the topic of your next book. It's a place to let your mind wander and think deep thoughts.

Idea #5: Use Wikipedia. Wikipedia gets a bad reputation because the content is not written by experts. Instead it relies on a series of volunteers, editors, and fact-checkers to crowdsource the content. The information is usually accurate, but there are times when it's completely wrong. All that said, Wikipedia can be used to do some research (like checking dates or names), but it shouldn't be the *only* part of your research

The one thing you should remember about Wikipedia is it's a good starting point, but you should always find reliable sources for any important facts that you include in your book.

Idea #6: Take lessons related to your topic. If an important aspect of your plot is related to a skill, then it makes sense to learn everything you can about it.

For instance, it's hard to write about a character riding a motorcycle if you have never done it yourself. Interviews with serious motorcycle aficionados can get you the details, but at some point, you should get on a motorcycle and ride it to truly understand and convey your character's viewpoint.

Idea #7: Watch instructional YouTube videos. The amount of information on YouTube is amazing. Here you can find makeup tips, do-it-yourself tutorials, medical information, and the "occasional" cat video. YouTube really does have it all. So if you need to quickly explain a concept, then you can learn enough by watching a video.

The final thing I have to say about research is that these facts are often for *your* benefit, not always for the readers. Sure, some facts can enrich your storytelling. But you shouldn't overload the reader with pages of exposition and pointless facts.

My advice is simple … Start with as much research as you think the reader needs and then brutally edit it down to a tight narrative. What you'll end up with is a great story that balances facts with a page-turning reading experience.

NOT-SO-OBVIOUS WRITING PRINCIPLE #4:

CREATING CONSISTENT CONTENT THAT READERS LOVE

Our society is obsessed with the idea of the *overnight success* where a person comes from nowhere and strikes it rich. It doesn't matter if it's an actor, musician, author, or lottery winner, these success stories make us all believe that *anything* is possible with a little bit of luck.

Unfortunately, overnight success is not possible for most writers. For every E. L. James (author of the Fifty Shades trilogy), there are hundreds of other authors who struggle with their careers. And the ones who do succeed do so because they take a workmanlike approach to their career and consistently publish new content.

My point here?

You should forget the idea that writing one book will lead to instant fame and success. Sure it happens from time to time. But it's like hitting the lottery, the winner is in the right place at the right time.

The secret to long-term writing success is to continuously produce and get better at your craft. Not only does this mean building the writing habit, it also means producing *something* on a regular basis—even if you don't publish all of your writing efforts.

Lessons from Successful Authors

There are countless examples of authors who succeed because they publish on a continual basis. To the casual observer, they might seem like overnight successes, but if you examine their daily habits, you'll see that they produced great content *way* before anybody noticed.

Here are a few examples:

John Irving published five unsuccessful books before penning *The World According to Garp,* which quickly became an international best seller.

Phillip Pullman produced 18 novels and achieved only moderate success until he wrote *The Golden Compass,* which kicked off the popular His Dark Materials trilogy.

Michael J Sullivan spent ten years writing a wide variety of books in a wide variety of genres. When he could not generate a single sale, he quit writing. Ten years later, he came back and self-published his Riyira Revelation fantasy series (which is *really* good, by the way). These books amassed solid sales numbers, and a traditional publisher bought the rights to these stories.

Hugh Howey was fortunate enough to land a traditionally publishing deal for his first few books, but they didn't sell well. His success came after self-publishing the novella Wool, which has led not only to a series of best-selling books, but also a movie option with Ridley Scott. (To learn more, check out this article where Hugh provides a wealth of advice to aspiring writers: tinyurl.com/ howeyadvice)

Take these examples to heart. It's a better to produce (and complete) content on a regular basis than to spend years working on the perfect novel. This teaches you both the discipline to see projects through to their conclusion, and how to improve your skills after receiving feedback from editors and readers.

As our own Honorée Corder shares in her book *Prosperity for Writers*, you must "BOLO" (be on the lookout) for examples, large and small, of successful writers who have gotten that way through consistent, persistent action.

To illustrate this point, let's talk about a speech that Ray Bradbury gave at the Point Loma Nazarene University's Writer's Symposium (tinyurl.com/bradburyplnu). He recommended that instead of starting with a novel, a new writer should take an entire year and produce 52 short stories, one for each week.

In Bradbury's view, it's impossible to write 52 bad short stories. Not only would this give you the confidence to complete writing projects on a regular basis, it would give you the opportunity to improve your craft over time.

Now, I'm not saying that writing 52 short stories is the only way to succeed. But the takeaway here is to consistently publish new content. It doesn't matter if you're publishing books, blog posts, or full-length novels, your writing journey starts by publishing content and having the mental strength to listen to honest feedback about what could be improved. As Steve Jobs once said, "Real artists ship."

So how do you actually publish content on consistent basis?

That's the question I'll answer in this chapter. What you'll learn is the nine-step process I use to manage and finish my writing projects, seeing each one through to completion

Step #1: Focus on One Project at a Time

If you're like me, then there are many ideas running around your head. You get excited about one thought, and you want to write about it *right now*—even if you're already working on something else.

The problem is this: When you start and stop a dozen projects, you're *not* completing a single thing. In fact, you're teaching yourself that it's okay to quit whenever a project becomes challenging or boring.

The lesson you can learn from top authors is that they succeed because they finish most of their projects—even when they feel frustrated or bored by the process.

To illustrate this point, let's talk about the differences between two authors:

Bob is a prolific writer, but he never finishes what he starts. In fact, he has 15 incomplete book projects. These include rough drafts of novels, opening chapters to books, and a few outlines of books that were never written. Sure, he has produced more words than the average person, but none have value because they haven't been published. Even worse, Bob has developed a negative attitude toward writing because he can't seem to complete a single project.

Now let's talk about Mary who has three published books. Her word count is significantly less than Bob's, but she always finishes what she starts.

More importantly, Mary's sales generate passive income each month from these books, and she often gets feedback (both positive and negative) from readers. While her career is just getting started, she is learning a lot about the publishing process from these early experiences.

My question to you is … which author will have more long-term success?

1. Bob, who has lots of great ideas, but never finishes.

2. Mary, who has three completed projects, but always finishes what she starts.

Hopefully you agree that Mary will have more long-term success. That's because she's a producer, not a dreamer.

Understand that real results come from completing writing projects on a continual basis. While it's okay to occasionally abandon ideas that aren't working, you should focus on completing the majority of what you start.

Step #2: Work on Your Belief System

Writing consistently (daily!) is a challenge without a doubt, yet it is entirely possible. Why, then, do many writers fall short when it comes to execution? Because it's impossible to exceed our internal belief systems, and if you don't believe it is possible to be a consistent creator of solid content, you simply won't. Therefore there are lots of aspiring writers who either don't believe they can write well, or they don't believe they can prosper as writers so they give up before they ever really start. Which is a shame, because there has never been better time to make a living as a writer (this means you!).

Every day the number of writers who are making a living through the various channels we explore in depth in this book increases. A critical difference between those who do and those who don't are the closely-held beliefs of the successful writers.

To upgrade your writing career from side-hustle to main gig means taking a hard look at what you believe is possible for you. Expanding your money consciousness will serve to expand your bank account.

I highly suggest including writing and success affirmations and visualization in your miracle morning practice, but also money and abundance specific affirmations and visualizations. You'll notice this is only number two in a decent-sized list of action items, because our belief about what is possible is changed one thought, word, and action at a time. If you'd like a simple yet very effective strategic approach to improving your internal beliefs (and eliminating those that simply don't work for you), check out *Prosperity for Writers*.

Step #3: Craft a Reader Avatar

An avatar isn't just a tall, blue alien from a James Cameron movie. It's also a detailed, fictional biography of your ideal reader. When crafting an avatar, you write a story that describes both the demographics and psychographics of a person who would be interested in checking out your writing.

How to Create a Reader Avatar

A good avatar comes from your personal interactions. While it's a fictional biography of a made-up person, most of the characteristics come from the conversations you've had with people about the problems in their lives (for nonfiction) and stories they enjoy (for fiction). This biography should answer a series of questions like

- Who is this person?

- What is his primary goal?

- What thoughts happen inside his head?

- What emotions does he regularly experience?

- What obstacles does he regularly encounter? Is it competition? Challenging technology? Limiting beliefs?

- What are his fears? (In other words, what keeps him up late at night?)

- What are the demographics of this reader? Age, race, sex, location, occupation, background, or interests?

You *don't need* to answer all of the above questions. Instead, focus on the ones that directly relate to your topic. For instance, when creating the avatar for this book (see below), I wasn't concerned so much with demographics because writing is related to an interest instead of a person's background.

Once you have one avatar clearly defined, create *multiple* avatars. We all have our unique challenges, so not everyone will response positively to the same message. It's a good idea to craft three to four avatar biographies and come up with a different message for each one.

As an example, there are (at least) two types of people who will buy *The Miracle Morning for Writers*. The first struggle with consistency and finding time for writing. The second group has no problem with hitting their daily word counts, but they have trouble turning this passion into a profitable hobby.

In preparation for this book, I had to craft multiple avatars and figure out the message for each group. If I was talking to an avatar from the first group, I would emphasize the importance of mini habits and not breaking the chain of consecutive days. But if I spoke with someone interested in monetizing their content, then I would talk about the various opportunities to sell their content through blogging, freelancing, and self-publishing. See why it's important to come up with multiple avatars?

The final step in creating your avatars is to use an alliterative name like Overtaxed Oliver, Techie Tina, or Habitual Henry. Not only will this make it easy to remember the description, it will also help you keep this perfect customer in mind as you're working on that next writing project.

Here is an example of a reader avatar that I created.

Journalist James

James is happily married with a two-year-old son and a daughter on the way. He has a full-time job as a journalist at a major city newspaper, but wants to do more with his writing. Specifically, he would like to make money by publishing a series of how-to books related to building a career in journalism.

The biggest challenge he faces is finding time to write. His job forces him to work long hours, and he has to meet deadlines on a daily basis. James also has a number of family and personal challenges that make it hard to create a consistent writing habit. For instance:

- *He wants to stay consistent with his Miracle Morning routine, which often eats into his writing time.*

- *He feels drained at the end of the day and doesn't have the energy to write.*

- *He often starts writing projects, but never sees them through to their conclusion.*

- *He has a limited amount of time, so he is looking for ways to increase his per-hour word count.*

- *He is a natural storyteller, but doesn't know how to parlay this into content that people who actually pay money want to read.*

Overall, James's main struggle is simple: he wants to write as much possible, but he doesn't know how to balance this activity with a dozen competing obligations.

Fortunately, he picks up a copy of The Miracle Morning for Writers *and discovers how to build a daily routine that focuses on consistent writing.*

As you can see, it's not that hard to craft a short avatar biography. It's simply a personification of the challenges that your average reader faces. You can use my example above to craft a biography that sounds like the perfect person for your content.

My last piece of advice is to write and print out this description for each of your writing projects. That way, you can keep your ideal reader in mind as you're working. And whenever you get stuck, just think about what would be the most useful (or entertaining) to this person.

Step #4: Identify Your Logline

It doesn't matter if you're writing a book, or screenplay, it's important to identify the *logline* before getting started. A logline is a few sentences long and provides a shorthand description of the writing project. This is similar to an elevator pitch that entrepreneurs use to briefly describe their business.

For instance, consider this popular description of *The Wizard of Oz* (tinyurl.com/j3qwqfa): "A lonely, young, small-town girl is swept away to a magical land by a tornado and embarks on a quest to see the Wizard who can help her return home."

Or you could describe *Getting Things Done* (a nonfiction book) as "A technique for organizing your projects, lists, and schedule into a daily, step-by-step strategy. It's a framework where you constantly evaluate all your obligations and make effective decisions on what to do next—without feeling distracted by the feeling of overwhelm from your other projects."

Or you could describe *The Miracle Morning for Writers* as "A system to build a powerful morning routine with the writing habit that teaches readers how to create great content on a consistent basis."

It's not hard to come up with a logline that summarizes content while creating a lot of curiosity in the reader's mind. Here is simple process for crafting that perfect logline for your next project.

First, ask the following questions for the nonfiction market:

- What common problems do people experience with this topic?

- What are the holes in the marketplace? What problems are largely ignored by other books?

- What step-by-step advice can you give the reader?

- What tools, resources, or websites are available to the reader?

- What expertise or knowledge can you add from your own personal experience?

- If you were starting out now with this topic, what would you like to know?

Now if you're a fiction writer, you can ask these questions instead:

- What are the common tropes in the genre that readers love?

- Can I combine two popular ideas to create something unique? (Like *Harry Potter* meets *On the Road:* a story about a young wizard and the people he encounters in his journey through the United States.)

- What point of view will be used? (First person or third person are the primary ones.)

- Where will the story be set?

- What characters will be included?

Questions like these are important because they help you come up with unique angles to add to your narrative. Sure, many ideas won't become part of the logline, but they are great for sparking those creative juices.

The next step is to craft a logline with your avatar in mind. Remember, you're trying to appeal to a certain type of reader. So this person should always be at the forefront of your mind, and the logline should captivate this person's attention.

The third step is to come up with *at least* a dozen loglines. Some might be completely unique ideas, while others could be similar to other books. The important thing is to jot down every thought that occurs to you.

Fourth, you should get feedback from readers and other writers. You could do this in a number of ways: poll your beta readers, ask for help in your writer's group, post updates on social media, or email your list. The more feedback you receive, the more you'll increase your chances of landing on an idea that resonates with your readers. (If you don't have a following yet, then be sure to check out Chapter Nine.)

The final step is to craft your logline. Remember that *you* are the person creating the content. So it should be a topic that is interesting to you *and* to your readers. My advice is to go with your gut and pick the logline that matches both requirements.

Step #5: Survey Potential Readers

Once you've identified your logline, poll your readers (again) and ask them to describe their biggest challenges and obstacles relating to your topic. This step is important because it shapes the direction of your book and addresses the most common problems that readers in your market encounter.

The simplest way to do this is to survey your readers. One strategy that I use is to start with as open-ended question like "What is your number one challenge with [the topic of your book]?" If you have a lot of followers, then you will receive a wealth of responses that will practically write your book for you.

Another suggestion is to look for common themes among these responses and then organize them into four to six buckets based on the similarity of the topics. This is a useful strategy because it identifies the different broad topics that should be covered in your content.

For example, when I polled my audience in preparation for *The Miracle Morning for Writers*, I noticed variations of these five basic questions:

1. How do I find time to write and complete *The Miracle Morning*?

2. How can I turn writing into a consistent habit?

3. How do I actually make money from this activity?

4. How can I complete my projects without getting distracted?

5. How do I overcome a lack of confidence in my writing?

As you can see, *all* of these topics are covered in this book. Hal, Honorée, and I didn't make assumptions about the needs of our readers. Instead, we polled our followers and identified the common challenges in their lives. And then all we had to do was create content that solved these specific issues.

Now, asking potential readers about their number one challenge is just one example of a question to ask your readers. You can ask other questions like these:

1. What should I write next? (Be sure to provide a few suggestions.)

2. What social media site do you prefer? (This can help you decide where to focus your social media activities.)

3. What are your favorite books or authors? (Maybe this will trigger an idea for what to write next.)

4. What is the best book you've read in the past year?

5. What do you think of this title or cover? (Great for getting honest feedback and building buzz about your next project)

6. Demographic questions (Age, sex, or location)

7. Psychographic questions (Interests, hobbies, or life goals)

How to Run a Survey

It's not hard to survey to a group of potential readers. In this section, I'll go over five strategies and which one to pick based on whether or not you have an existing audience.

1. Leverage Your Platform. If you have a blog, podcast, YouTube channel, or a sizeable social media following, then these followers already know, like, and trust you. So they should be the first people you turn to whenever you need honest feedback on an idea.

2. Send an Email to Your List. While leveraging your platform is a great first step, a better option is to poll your email list. My suggestion is to send an open-ended question that encourages subscribers to share their pains, frustrations, and challenges with your topic area.

If you have time, try to respond to each message. Yes, this can be a very time-consuming process, but it's a great way to build a solid relationship with subscribers, one person at a time.

Another recommendation is to collect each response into a folder that's dedicated to this writing project. These contacts will be useful when you're about to publish and you need beta readers or reviews. You can email each person with a simple request and most will help out since they've *already* made a partial commitment to the project.

3. Ask Questions in Social Media Groups. Sites like Facebook, LinkedIn, or Google Plus have communities for every imaginable topic. When you find a group related to your next writing project, you can tap into a pool of potential readers who have *already* demonstrated an interest in your topic. All you have to do is start asking the right questions.

One thing to remember about social media is you shouldn't join a group and immediately ask a bunch of questions. Instead your goal is to make connections, answer members' questions, and build a positive reputation. Then, once you've become a trusted expert, you can start a thread asking people about their challenges.

4. Interact in Niche Specific Forums. Online forums are another great resource because members are *already* interested in your topic. The trick to these sites is to understand what type of content members are allowed to post. Some forums allow self-promotion, while others will immediately delete your threads or even your account if you do. So take time to understand the rules before posting anything.

5. Post on Reddit. Reddit (Reddit.com) is a social news networking site. The content is completely user driven, with a strong emphasis on limiting self-promotional material. This means if you post something that users don't like, there will be a negative backlash.

Fortunately, there are numerous Reddit categories (called "subreddits") that allow you to poll members and promote your book. Take time to read the posted rules for *each* subreddit. These will detail what you can post, how to post it, and other rules for interacting with readers. My advice is to read and understand these rules before getting started with any new subreddit.

Four Tools for Running Surveys

Most surveys are informal where you ask an open-ended question and see how people respond. But if you want to add a level of sophistication (and automation), then you can use software that manages the process. Here are four tools that I've used and highly recommend:

1. Survey Monkey (surveymonkey.com) is good for multiple choice questions and getting demographic information about your audience, like age, sex, or occupation. It's a great starting point if you have a following, but you don't know what to include in your reader avatar.

2. Survey Gizmo (surveygizmo.com) is similar to Survey Monkey because it allows you to ask multiple choice questions. The big difference here is you can also ask open-ended questions and collate these responses into an easy to understand document. If you want to ask broad questions and allow readers to respond anonymously, then this is the service for you.

3. PickFu (pickfu.com) allows you to poll 50 to 200 people (from their database of users) to help you make an important decision, like picking a new topic, cover image, or book title. The benefit here is each respondent has to leave a comment about their voting choice. So not only do you get a vote on an important decision, you also get many honest opinions about your writing project. Often these comments will identify a major issue that you might not have originally considered.

4. WP Polls (tinyurl.com/h5w6grs) is a quick, free plugin you can install on any WordPress enabled site. It's not fancy, but it allows you to ask simple questions and get instant feedback from your audience.

One thing to keep in mind is that you need to invest time and money to survey potential readers. It's tempting to skip this part of the process. But I think you should never *assume* that you know what your audience wants. Often a simple poll will reveal a lot of golden opportunities that you never considered before. Do this before every major project, and you will become a writer who provides great content on a consistent basis.

Book Recommendation

Want to learn more about the power of surveying your audience? I recommend reading *Ask* by Ryan Levesque. Inside this book, you will learn things like how to communicate with potential customers, use surveys to find out what they want, and then create products that best serve their needs.

While *Ask* is written primarily for business owners, there are a number of golden nuggets you can use to take your writing business to the next level. It's perfect for anyone who has an existing audience but is struggling with identifying what they really want.

Step #6a: Create an Outline (Nonfiction)

There are two types of writers: *plotters* who plan out their writing with an outline or story beats and *pantsers* who sort of know what they want to write, but come up with the content as they dive into the writing project.

I won't argue about the merits of one over the other. But in this step, I will describe how plotting can help you take a simple idea and turn it into a full-length book.

The first step of the process is to do research and brainstorm for *at least* a few days. If you've been using Evernote regularly, then you've probably added a number of ideas to your book-related notebook in the app. My advice is to continue to add to this folder before starting your writing project.

How much research you do depends on the depth of the content you're covering. Obviously, if your book requires an extensive amount of research, quotes, interviews, and fact-checking, then you might need a month (or more) to complete your research. On the other hand, if you're writing a "how-to" book based on skills you've mastered, then you might need only a few days.

The next step is to take this research and do a brainstorming session. Basically, this is where you set aside a few hours to *hand-write* everything that will be included in the book. The key here is to free your mind and connect one idea with another idea.

During this brainstorming session make sure you:

- Avoid correcting spelling or grammar.

- Jot down even incomplete seeds of ideas.

- Avoid censoring any idea, even if it seems stupid or irrelevant.

- Make notes like "research this idea" if you don't know much about a random thought.

- Don't worry about how you'll work a particular idea into the book or if it even fits.

The goal of a brainstorming session is to write down a large number of ideas. So if you get stuck and can't think of anything else to include, then take some time off (or switch to another book-business related task) and start again the next day. The important thing is to keep writing down your thoughts until you have pages of content that will form the backbone of your next book.

After completing this session, take these ideas and turn them into a framework that will become your outline. The best way to do this is to buy a pack of index cards (like the 3x5 Oxford ruled cards) and use them to map out the skeleton of your writing project.

To get started, identify the 8 to 12 big ideas for your book. These will represent the major breaks in the content and will often become the chapters. Write down these ideas on the blank side of an index card.

One suggestion is to turn each idea into a simple question that you will answer within that chapter. For instance, the question that I created for this section is "how do you take an idea and turn it into a publish-ready book?"

Next, go through the other ideas in your brainstorming document. You will write each down on a different index card (also on the blank side) and organize them into one of the 8 to 12 chapter stacks you've already mapped out. At this point, you will have anywhere from 24 to 48 index cards, each representing a chapter or subchapter of your book.

Third, take each index card that represents a subchapter, flip over to the lined side and flesh out the topic by adding a few ideas you want to cover. Here you'll add all the material from your research and notes you've put into Evernote. This is where you'll add quotes, case studies, personal anecdotes, or website links.

You don't have to write full sentences on these index cards. Put enough information to spark your creativity when you're working on the first draft.

Finally, you should do a quick review of these index cards to make sure the narrative has a logical flow. You will do a few things here:

- Shuffle the ideas if you don't think they work in a specific section.

- Cross out anything that doesn't work for your hook or reader avatar.

- Get rid of redundant ideas or combine good ideas to make one strong point instead of three repetitive and weak points.

- Rip up cards that simply don't work for your book.

- Highlight areas where you need to do research or come up with more supporting evidence.

- Make notes to yourself about adding illustrations, coming up with metaphors, or otherwise fleshing out an idea.

Now, I do realize that using index cards to map out a book *seems* like extra work, but it's a great strategy to organize your ideas into a logical flow. It's also the best way to prevent writer's block because you'll never be in a position where you're wondering what to write because the next topic has already been identified!

Step #6b: Create Your Beats (Fiction)

Creating beats is what fiction writers do to outline their books. It's a similar process to nonfiction because you will have mapped out the story line. The way it's different from nonfiction is that you need to focus on what characters learn and how the narrative flows from one scene to another.

There are many different types of story beats or ways to outline your story with varying levels of detail. When creating the framework for your book, you should identify what you will write for each of the following:

Story Beats are an outline of the external events that happen in a story and describe what will happen in a particular chapter or scene.

They often look like this: X happens, which causes Y to happen. The fact that Y occurred causes the protagonist to do A, which of course results in B.

A key component of story beats is to make sure the events in the narrative happen when they are supposed to. But isn't every story different? Yes, but people have been telling stories for thousands of years, and readers expect certain events at a particular time in the story. For example, the main character usually experiences a reversal of fortune at the midpoint of the story, and there is an all is lost moment before the climax when it looks as if things won't work out.

Emotional Beats, sometimes called the character arc, focus on the growth of the main character(s) that occurs as a result of the external events of the story.

For example, a character may start out being a materialistic jerk. He then might experience major financial setbacks that force him to examine his materialism and make different choices. This new perspective might bring about an emotional change in the character. By the end of the story, he *might* regain his wealth, but he will behave differently because he has a new appreciation for the financial struggles that other people go through.

A Christmas Carol by Charles Dickens is a great example of a story like this.

In the beginning of the story, Scrooge hates Christmas and lacks empathy for the people in his life. He is visited by Jacob Marley's ghost and the ghosts of Christmas past, present, and future. Each meeting creates conflict that allows Scrooge to gain a new perspective on the importance of the people in his life and the consequences of his actions.

In the final scenes, the reader sees the results of Scrooge's transformation when he wakes up on Christmas morning. He focuses on rebuilding those lost connections he has ignored in the past, marking his emotional change.

Scene Beats focus on the important elements in your scenes, including dialogue and actions. As a writer, you don't have to map out everything that takes place in a scene, but you should at least identify the major things that need to happen or be said.

Combining All Three

Your beats or story outline should include the events of the global story, the emotional or inner journey of the main character, and the events and dialogue of the individual scenes.

If you want to learn more about what a well-designed story beat structure looks like, then I recommend checking out *The Story Grid* by Shawn Coyne, which shows you how to take an analytical approach to your narrative and make sure you're hitting the important points of the plot.

This is a book on editing, but one that, along with the podcast can help a writer make the most of the rough draft. Knowing what needs to be included in the story for it to work (for example obligatory scenes and conventions in the global story and increasing complications within scenes) will help you get those elements on the page during the first draft.

Step 6: Write Your "Crappy" First Draft

Throughout *The Miracle Morning for Writers*, I've talked about strategies for overcoming writer's block. What you've learned is it's often caused by those internal, limiting beliefs that make you second guess your skill as a writer. Unfortunately, these thoughts often rear their ugly heads while you're writing your first draft. So sometimes you'll get stuck on a section and suddenly feel like you don't have the skills to be a successful writer.

The solution to this form of writer's block is simple: you need to write the first draft *without* trying to edit it.

Just think back to what we discussed in Chapter Four. When it comes to creating content, you need to access two parts of your brain.

The creative side of your brain helps you think of plots, ideas, and important points. You will need to access the creative side of your brain when you are writing your outline and your rough drafts.

The editing side of your brain is hypercritical and often gets in the way of producing creative work. While it's an *essential* part of writing, you shouldn't worry about this side of your brain until you've completed the first draft.

My point here is simple …

You can't create good content and edit at the same time!

Many writers get stuck in the first draft because they try to write the perfect manuscript right off the bat. They fear bad writing, so they will waste hours tweaking and editing a page of content instead of focusing on coming up with original thoughts. Your challenge is to ignore the critical editor part of your brain that tempts you to stop and tweak the copy as you write.

Instead, you need to remind yourself of an important truth:

The quality of your first draft *doesn't* matter. What matters is *completing* it.

Believe it or not, the first draft should be the easiest part of the writing process. (The hard part comes later.) Your goal is to take the content on your index cards (the outline or beats) and elaborate on what you've already mapped out. Here are a few ways to do this:

- Add content to each point you've listed in the outline.

- Skip over sections where you can't think of anything to write.

- Ignore spelling, grammar, or fact-checking. All of these will be fixed in the next few drafts.

- Write notes to yourself about what you need to do to make this chapter work. (Use comments in your word processing software if you don't like to include it in the text.)

- Include more content than you think is necessary, knowing you will edit much of it out later.

As you write, you will hit points where you don't know what to say next. Instead of agonizing over these rough patches, create a reminder to go back over it and then skip to the next section. The key here is to not stop your writing before your session is up. You're just trying to get this draft down as quickly as possible, knowing the content will be cleaned up in later drafts.

How to Silence the "Editor Brain"

Often, you will be tempted to go back and revise certain sections while working on your first draft. This is a perfectly normal impulse that every writer experiences. But this is the moment when you need to silence that inner critic. Simply remind yourself that

- "This is just a rough draft. It's not supposed to be good."

- "It's a work in progress. I'm supposed to have holes and incomplete thoughts."

- "I am the only person who will see this draft. I don't need to worry about what anyone else will think."

One of the best pieces of advice I've heard about silencing your inner critic comes from Stephen King. In his book, *On Writing*, King recommends writing your rough drafts with the "door closed" because it gives you a psychological boost. In other words, assume that no one but you will read that draft. You can make mistakes in private and not feel that you need to get everything right the first time around.

Step 7: Revise with a Second Draft

Your second draft is the time to shift gears to the editor brain. Your job is take the rough copy and turn it a polished narrative.

It's also important to make sure your content matches what readers expect in your chosen market.

For **nonfiction books**, be sure that you have

- Identified the core problem that your book solves or the overall premise at the start of the book.

- Demonstrated your authority. Answer the question, how are you uniquely qualified to provide advice on this subject?

- Described common obstacles, including the challenges the readers face or the limiting beliefs.

- Provided actionable content. This includes step-by-step processes, checklists, bullet points, and simple how-to information. (For a good example, just look at how we organized the content in this book.)

- Included stories that describe experiences that you (and others) have gone through related to the topic.

- Used scenarios that explain the concept in terms of where the reader is in that situation. These are the statements that start with "Imagine you are …" or "Think of a time when you …"

- Provided links to websites, resources, and downloads that help the reader get more information on the topic.

- Added images that perfectly illustrate an important lesson.

Another important aspect of effective nonfiction is to structure the content so readers can quickly scan the information. The truth is it's *really* hard to read large blocks of text. Breaking it up is a good way to please both the folks who read every word *and* the scanners who simply want to understand the major concepts.

My recommendation is to use

- Short words, short sentences, and short paragraphs.

- Eight to twelve chapters separated by page breaks. Also be sure that you cover *only* one major topic within each chapter.

- Headlines that identify different concepts within each chapter. If a section has more than five paragraphs of unbroken text, then add a header that best summarizes the concept.

- Bullet points, numbered lists, and text boxes whenever you have to make more than five points about a topic (like I did with this list).

You can make the argument that *real* readers don't need dumbed down content. But keep in mind that your book is in competition with hundreds—even thousands—of others in your market. So if you make it easy to read and absorb your content, you'll increase the likelihood that they'll finish the book and recommend it, which has a positive, long-term impact on getting those repeat readers.

The second draft for **fiction books** is a little different. Instead of educating, your goal is to entertain. This means your job is to draw the reader into the story and help him slip into your fictional world. So while it's still important to edit for grammar and spelling, it's *more* important to examine the entire story and ask yourself these questions:

- How does this scene move the plot along?

- How does each scene connect to the others?

- Am I being consistent with my descriptions? (Character eye color, background, personality, etc.)

- Do the events of the story justify the changes in the main character?

- Is my story following the conventions and pacing for the chosen genre? (Action for thrillers, emotional tension for romance, or a unique setting for fantasy)

Overall, the goal of the second draft of your story is to make sure that the narrative is consistent and the readers are engaged and fully immersed in the story. So for every decision that you make during this process, you should keep these things in mind.

Finally, here are a number of actions to complete while working on the second draft for both a fiction and nonfiction book:

- Reword awkward sentences

- Simplify long paragraphs

- Cut extra words

- Check facts

- Add hyperlinks

- Flesh out empty spots

- Insert examples

- Move around blocks of text

- Cut anything that doesn't fit

- Check grammar rules

- Fix any spelling mistakes

Don't worry if a second draft takes longer than the first draft. This often happens because you take the time to tweak the content to make sure it provides a quality reading experience. It's also the point where you agonize over every word, sentence, and paragraph. The good news is most of the content is *already* written, so you won't need a lot of creative energy to create tight copy.

Step 8: Proofread the Third Draft

Your job during the second draft is to do a structural edit to make sure the content logically flows from one section to the next. Your job in the third draft is to add a final polish and ready your manuscript to be sent to an editor. There are three actions you should complete with this step:

#1: Tighten the Text

It doesn't matter if it's a fiction or nonfiction piece—the book probably contains too much material. Your goal is to provide a great reading experience, so assess your draft and eliminate anything that isn't needed. This means doing another pass where you simplify the language, cut out extraneous words and eliminate "fluff" sections that aren't crucial to the narrative.

My recommendation here is to "kill your darlings," which is common advice given to aspiring writers. This means deleting what's unimportant—even if it's a section that you personally love. Your job is to keep the reader in mind and be a brutal as possible.

#2: Read the Narrative Aloud

It's easy to make simple, grammatical mistakes in your writing. The best way to catch them is to read your book aloud and note the sections that sound awkward. Not only will this help you correct those small mistakes, it will also give you an opportunity to revise the dialogue until it sounds natural to your ears.

Another benefit is you will identify areas where a concept wasn't fully explained or maybe where a scene needs to be fleshed out. By reading the book out loud, you give yourself a chance to catch those areas that need to be smoothed out.

#3: Add the Extra Material

You also need to include sections to the front and back of the book like:

- A title page
- Dedication and acknowledgments
- Links to free resources (I'll talk about this in the next section.)
- Quotes that relate to important concepts
- Images and illustrations
- Bibliography or a resources section
- A list of your other books

How much content you add depends on the book project. The important thing to keep in mind is the overall reading experience. Provide helpful information and a way for your readers to connect with you, but avoid filling your books with dozens of pages of fluff and marketing materials.

My suggestion is to keep this question in the back of your mind: *How will this section improve the quality of my book?*

If you don't have a good answer to this question, then keep that section out of your book.

At this point, you've worked hard on your book—writing and revising it through multiple drafts. The next required step is one of the most important in the entire process, but it's often ignored by many aspiring authors. So let's talk next about why working with an editor is a critical part of the publishing process.

Step 9: Work with an Editor

It doesn't matter if you're a great writer—you should *always* work with an editor on your important writing projects.

The value of a good edit is immeasurable. Not only will this person provide a critique of the content, she also acts as a second pair of eyes to catch those small mistakes that you didn't notice in your previous revisions.

When hiring an editor, you look for someone who

- Is well-versed in English, someone who understands all the grammar rules, but also understands your logic for breaking certain conventions.

- Has worked in your genre or niche.

- Can prioritize your book so you're not waiting months for their feedback.

- Provides detailed information that can help you grow as a writer.

Your editor will become *the* most important member of your team. So my recommendation is to work with a few different people until you find the right person. It's okay to take your time here because you want to work with a trusted advisor you can turn to whenever you have a writing-related question.

So you might ask, *"Where do I find a great editor?"*

Here are a five places where you can look:

1. Social media: If you're in an online writer's group, then ask for specific recommendations from members who are familiar with your work and know an editor that has experience in this niche or genre.

2. Leslie Watts is the main editor of this book. You can connect with her and learn more about her editing services by visiting LeslieWattsEditor.com.

3. KBoards.com is one of the largest forums for indie published authors. You can ask for referrals for editors that authors have successfully used in the past.

4. Upwork (upwork.com) is one the largest websites for finding freelance talent. Simply post a job here, and you'll get a large number of bids from qualified editors. This is the site that I've personally used to hire two great editors.

5. Reedsy (reedsy.com) is helpful for hiring high-caliber designers and editors. It's different from other freelance websites because each freelancer has been fully vetted by the Reedsy team. This will help you to be sure that the editor you're working with actually has the qualifications to provide help.

No matter where you find an editor, the key thing to remember is to work with someone who understands the scope of your project, is familiar with your market, and can provide in-depth feedback that will help you grow as writer.

Three Types of Editing

There are many ways an editor can improve your book and your writing. But it's easy to get confused about what you need before hiring someone. That's why I recommend understanding the different types of editing and why each one is an important part of taking your manuscript from a rough draft to a final draft:

A developmental or content editor provides structural advice on your book. This editor should look at the big picture to make sure the narrative flows, whether fiction or nonfiction, in a logical way. She looks for plot holes and scenes that don't fit and provides a critique on the pacing of a story.

A copy editor will look at how you have conveyed your ideas or story and smooth out the language while also fixing your spelling, punctuation, and grammar mistakes.

A proofreader is usually the last person to check your book before it's published. She is responsible for checking every line and catching mistakes in language and factual consistency that weren't noticed in previous passes.

While all three types of editors are important, most aspiring authors can't afford to pay for all of them. So if you're just getting started, then you can eliminate some of the cost by joining writer groups and getting feedback on your structure (to replace the developmental editing). Then you can hire an editor to copyedit and proofread to correct language errors and put a final polish on the book.

How much you need to invest in editing depends on the project and whom you hire. I recommend shopping around and using the sites I mentioned above. You should also understand what is considered to be a standard rate for the different types of editing services. To give you an idea of the costs, check out this rate scale provided by the Editorial Freelancers Association (tinyurl.com/editorrates).

The cost of working with an editor can be significant. But I'd consider it to be the best investment you can make for your writing business. Editing contributes to a positive reader experience, and positive reading experiences cause people to recommend and read more of your books. Even if you have a limited budget, I recommend spending as much money as you can afford.

Step 10: Publish Your Manuscript

The final step is to publish your writing project. Nowadays, this is a simple process that only takes a few minutes of your time. All you need to do is upload it to Amazon.com or post it to your content website. Or if you want to traditionally publish your book, then you can pitch your book to an agent. Bottom line—you now have *many* options when it comes to selling your book.

Since you have a few different options with this final step, I'll go over each one in the next chapter. Not only will I show you how to get started, I will also provide a recommendation of the one business model that every aspiring writer should try.

— 8 —

NOT-SO-OBVIOUS WRITING PRINCIPLE #5:

MONETIZING YOUR WORDS

The simplest way to measure the value of your writing is to see if people—especially random strangers—are willing to pay money for it. Even if making money isn't a major priority for you, there is no better feeling than experiencing that rush of seeing royalties from the hard work you've put into a piece of content.

Not only is it motivating to generate writing-related income, you also have the potential to replace your day job. The possibilities are endless when it comes to this business model.

We now live in an amazing time for writers. Now more than ever it's possible to identify a market, write to this audience, and earn a steady income by serving their needs. You probably won't earn at J. K. Rowling levels, but there is potential to earn a nice midlist income that matches a paycheck you would typically receive at a job. (There are thousands of writers who are doing this right now.)

There are countless ways to make money as a writer. But for the sake of brevity, I will cover the top four business models in this section:

1. Freelance Writing

2. Blogging

3. Traditional Publishing

4. Self-Publishing

Each has its advantages and disadvantages, and your choice will depend on your interests and goals. So let me go over the four business models and show how you can get started with each. Then you can make a decision on what works best for your personal situation.

Writing Opportunity #1: Freelance Writing

Freelance writing is the quickest way to make money with your words. Instead of starting a business from scratch, you can offer copywriting, ghostwriting, or services to help other writers and businesses.

The biggest advantage of freelancing is speed of implementation. Instead of spending months building a business (like you would with the other three models), you can bid on a project today and get paid by the end of the week. It's the perfect choice for anyone who just wants to earn a little bit of money on the side.

There are many sites where you can promote your freelancing writing services. Here are the biggest in the marketplace:

1. Upwork (upwork.com)

2. Craigslist (Look under the "writing" section of specific cities.)

3. Problogger Job Board (jobs.problogger.net)

4. Paid to Blog (jobs.paidtoblog.co)

5. Contena (contena.co)

6. BloggingPro Job Board (BloggingPro.com/jobs)

7. Online Writing Jobs (online-writing-jobs.com)

8. Freelance Writing Gigs (freelancewritinggigs.com)

9. Freelance Switch Jobs board (jobs.freelancewitch.com)

10. All Indie Writers (allindiewriters.com)

11. Journalism Jobs (JournalismJobs.com)

The biggest mistake that freelancers make is to rely solely on these job boards for work. To get consistent business, you need to differentiate yourself by building a collection of happy clients. Not only will your income become more reliable, you will get more clients as you gain word-of-mouth referrals.

If you're interested in freelance writing and want clients to come to you, then here is a four-step process for getting started.

Step 1: Create a Simple Website

You need a place where clients can find you and learn more about what you offer. Don't freak out if you're a technophobe, though. It's not that hard to build a website. More importantly, you won't need hundreds of web pages to promote your services. Really, the goal of a website is to showcase the quality of your work and to give potential clients a chance to get to know you better.

Here's what to include on your website:

1. Information about the writing market you specialize in (You'll get more work if you "niche-down.")

2. The onboarding process you use for new clients

3. Examples of previous projects you've worked on

4. Testimonials from clients

5. Your email address or a contact form

6. Links to your social media accounts

That's all you need for a basic website. You can add more if you want to, but most potential clients care only about your writing ability and experience with their industry. Don't overthink things. Instead, keep your website focused on these key pieces of information.

Step 2: Specialize in a Type of Freelance Work

It might seem counterintuitive, but the best way to get consistent work (and eventually raise your rates) is to specialize in one type of writing. By specializing in a particular area, you will become the go-to expert for people who need copy written on the subject.

For instance, if you are a writer who focuses on the fitness industry, then you will get a lot more repeat business and long-term work than a freelancer who bids on every possible job.

The benefit of specialization is that you build word-of-mouth buzz. Past clients will refer other clients and you'll build a name in this industry. Moreover, the more you educate yourself and write on the topic, the higher rates you will be able to charge.

There are tens of thousands of available writers in the world, but the people who generate the biggest income are the ones who master the knowledge of a specific industry.

Step 3: Maintain a Client Email List

Your success hinges on repeat business. This means you should keep a list of previous clients and maintain consistent contact. Sure, a previous client might not have any work to offer now, but that might change a few months down the road. Don't be scared to occasionally ping customers and ask if they need help with their latest projects. Or, better yet, find ways to offer value with monthly writing tips, for example. This will help distinguish you from the competition and keep your business first in the client's mind.

My recommendation is to create a spreadsheet and add the following for each customer:

- Name
- Email address
- The type of project you worked on
- Their birthday or any other personal information you can glean

You don't have to go overboard with staying connected to clients. Simply set a reminder every quarter to follow up with these people to see if they have any new projects.

Step 4: Focus on Client Acquisition

Landing new clients is an important part of the freelancing process. While you need to maintain relationships with previous clients, you should dedicate time every day to generate new leads for your business. Here are a few ways to do this:

- Ask for referrals from previous clients (these are the best kind of leads).

- Leverage freelancing websites as a way to prove your talent, and then follow up with these business to see if they need more work.

- Email websites and businesses in your niche to see if they need quality content to promote their product.

- Write guest posts on high-traffic websites and link to your services.

- Create a content marketing channel, solve people's problems, and use this content to demonstrate your knowledge in this area.

A great example of creating content to promote a freelance service is the *Writership* website. The site provides excellent advice through the podcast, books, and blog posts. And naturally people who enjoy the content will turn to *Writership* when they need help with a project because they've already received value from the free information.

Freelancing is the best way to generate immediate income with your writing. Sure, it's not as glamourous as seeing your book at the top of a best sellers list, but it's a good starting point for aspiring writers. If you simply don't have the time to write a book (or build a business), then freelancing might be a great starting opportunity.

Writing Opportunity #2: Blogging

Blogging is a viable business model for writers because you already have the one skill that many others don't possess—an ability to put words together and share your thoughts with the world.

But, before you jump into blogging, it's important to understand that it's very a long-term business model. For every six-figure blogger you read about, there are hundreds of bloggers who struggle to generate a few hundred dollars a month. What separates the successful from the not-so-successful is that the former focuses on building what's called an authority site. An authority site consists of a content-filled blog that focuses on a single topic and builds up repeat readership through consistent, quality content. You can break down the process of building this type of site into four steps.

Step #1: Pick a Niche

If your blog is filled with a collection of random thoughts, then it won't be successful. Remember, the best authority sites focus on a specific market, which relates to a problem, passion, or personal interest of an audience.

For instance, here are a few topics that relate to my personal interests:

- Running
- Hiking
- Traveling
- Parenting
- Personal Finance
- Politics
- Entrepreneurship
- Writing
- Self-Publishing
- Gadgets and Technology

These topics relate either to a personal passion or a skill that I want to master. The reason that I listed them here is to show that we all have varied interests. So if you closely examine your life, you'll find that it's not hard to pinpoint a topic that you can get excited about and that can be turned into a great authority site.

Step #2: Create Great Content

"Write epic content" is a buzz phrase that people love to say when it comes to blogging. But it's important to remember that there are over two billion websites on the Internet, and the only way to stand out is to provide real value to your readers. Not only will this help you gain the attention of an audience, it will make your job easier when you want to start monetizing your website.

What epic content means depends on your topic and personal interest. Often it's a mixed-bag of lengthy blog posts and short articles. Ideally, you want to include the following in your blog:

- Detailed how-to articles
- Fun numbered list articles (often called "listcles") focused on a common theme
- Definitions of niche-specific terms
- Roundup posts from other niche experts
- Reviews of tools, gadgets, or services

Each type of article serves a different purpose. Some, like the how-to article, provide step-by-step content that readers can use to improve their lives. Others, like listicles, are used to build buzz on social media sites. And a few, like the review articles, can help you generate income through affiliate relationships. The key here is to blend these articles together in a way that best serves the needs of your audience.

Here's an example:

Think back to the list of my personal interests. If I wanted to create an authority site about running, then I could write articles like these:

- How to Train for Your First Marathon (how-to)

- 21 Lightning-Fast Courses to Qualify for the Boston Marathon (listicle)

- What is a Fartlek Run? (definition)

- 23 Experts Share Their #1 Tip for Training in Harsh Winter Climates (roundup post)

- FitBit Blaze—The Complete Review for Runners (review)

The average person won't be interested in these topics. But if you're into running, then these articles would be compelling because they directly relate to obstacles and problems that you've probably experienced.

Step #3: Build Relationships

You can't blog in isolation. In fact, your growth is often determined by how well you interact with other bloggers and connect with their audiences.

Now, this isn't a strategy you can shortcut. You can't simply email a popular blogger and expect him to share your website with his audience. Instead, you need to do a few things to earn recognition in this crowded marketplace.

- Create in-depth guest posts for the top blogs in your niche

- Engage in topic-specific forums and social media groups that have lots of members

- Answer questions on Quora.com and link back to your site

- Respond to all questions and comments from people who visit your site

- Create good content that comes from these questions

- Do podcast and blog interviews for popular content websites

All of these strategies will take time. But if you do one action every day—maybe as an activity scheduled after your Miracle Morning—you will slowly get attention from your ideal audience.

Step #4: Explore Monetization Methods

Notice how "make money" is the last step in this process? This was done intentionally because when you focus on providing value first, it will be easier to generate long-term income than if you rush the process by creating a spammy website that doesn't serve the needs of an audience.

Fortunately, there are a number of options for monetizing your authority site. Some are easy to do, while others require hours of additional time to fully execute. In this final step, I will go over four proven models for generating income.

I. Display Advertising

This is the easiest way to make money with a brand new site, but it also has the worst long-term income potential. With display advertising, you add a piece of code into sections of your website, and you make money whenever visitors click one of these ads.

Here are the top sites that offer display advertising:

- Google Adsense (Google.com/Adsense)
- Media.net
- Buy Sell Ads (buysellads.com)
- Advertising.com
- Criteo (criteo.com)
- GumGum (gumgum.com)
- Collective Display (collective.com)

Since display advertising is the easiest way to make money, you might be tempted to place a dozen ads on your site and try to maximize your clicks. I recommend that you not do this! Instead, keep your readers in mind when it comes to advertising. While it's okay to place a few ads in key locations, you first want a great reading experience where visitors will keep coming back. And often, being too aggressive with display ads gets in the way of this goal.

II. Affiliate Marketing

Affiliate marketing can be a very lucrative way to make money. In fact, my full-time income from 2006 through 2012 came from this business model.

The premise of affiliate marketing is simple. There are hundreds of thousands of businesses that need customers for their products. One way these companies gain attention is to work with affiliates who will actively promote the offer to their audiences. If an affiliate recommendation leads to a sale, then the business gives the affiliate a percentage of the earnings. Often, this can be as high as 50-100 percent of the sales price.

In a way, affiliate marketing is similar to sales because you generate commission-based income and only make money when someone buys an offer. You need to be able to explain the features, understand a person's needs, and show the benefits of using the product.

The best affiliate marketers promote only the products they've used themselves. These offers should align with your authority brand and also provide a solution to a challenge your audience frequently encounters. That's how you stand out from the bloggers who worry more about the money they generate instead of the value they provide.

If you're interested in learning more about this income model, here are a few affiliate networks where you can find thousands of offers to promote:

- Amazon Associates (affiliate-program.amazon.com)
- Commission Junction (cj.com)
- LinkShare (LinkShare.com)
- Clickbank (clickbank.com)
- ShareaSale (sharesale.com)
- PeerFly (peerfly.com)

Another way to find a quality affiliate offer is to look at your favorite products or services. Investigate whether the provider has a self-hosted affiliate program that's easy to join. Most of the time, all you need to do is fill out a form and explain how you'll promote their offer. Then you'll be able to give a powerful recommendation to your audience because you're talking about a product that you know, like, and trust.

While affiliate marketing requires hard work, it's way more lucrative than display advertising. You build a lot of trust as you create valuable content for your audience. Then you can leverage this trust by promoting quality offers that not only serve their needs, but also put a sizeable commission in your pocket. Even if you decide to focus on any of the other three business models, I recommend promoting affiliate offers of products that you frequently use.

III. Coaching, Consulting, or Freelancing

If you offer a service (like coaching, consulting, or freelancing), then a blog is a great way to provide value and market your material to your ideal customer. Not only will you become a trusted expert in this industry, you will also land more customers because you've already proved your knowledge in this field.

Top coaches, consultants, and freelancers can earn six- and even seven-figure incomes. The challenge with providing services is that you must trade time for money and constantly network and market to gain new business. But a blog, or even a book, can position you to earn larger fees and help clients find you, especially when the content of either or both is carefully curated.

IV. Online Courses

This is the most challenging of the four income models, but it's also the most lucrative. Since you've built (or will build) an authority site, you're probably an expert on a specific topic. You turn your knowledge into an online course where customers learn from your experience.

Online education is a booming industry. People want to learn specific skills in an environment that fits their busy lifestyle. So if you get a lot of questions from your blog readers, then chances are good that you can package your knowledge into a series of lessons and sell it directly to your audience.

You have two basic options when it comes to creating online courses.

First, you can use a site like Udemy (udemy.com) (which has over 10 million users) to tap into an existing market and generate immediate income. This is the easiest option because you won't need an audience before getting started.

One negative aspect of Udemy you should take into account is that you have little control over your product's price. Not only do they force you to sell your course at $20-$50, they also run promotional discounts on their offers—often without your permission. So, while this site is a great way to leverage an existing marketplace, publishing here means you'll have little control over the product that *you* created. (But you still have the option to publish a course with Udemy to get started and then put it on your own platform when you want to scale up your business.)

The second option is to sell directly to your followers. This is a great alternative to Udemy if you have a large audience and want to maintain control over your intellectual property.

I'll admit that creating a course from scratch sounds scary because you have to master a number of technical challenges. Fortunately, there are a few websites that simplify the process and make the process as easy as uploading files to a website. My suggestion is to check out either Teachable (teachable.com) or Zippy Courses because they have streamlined the process for creating and selling (zippycourses.com) online courses by removing a lot of the technological headaches that often happen when you sell a course.

Like I said before, online education is a growing industry that's only creating more opportunities as more people expect on-demand, instant gratification information. If your authority site is filled with quality content, then you can generate a reliable income by packaging this information in a step-by-step course.

How to Get Started with Authority Sites

I've barely scratched the surface of what's possible with building an authority site. If you're interested in this business model, then I recommend five websites that will walk you through the entire process:

1. Authority Hacker (AuthorityHacker.com)
2. Niche Pursuits (NichePursuits.com)
3. Smart Passive Income (SmartPassiveIncome.com)
4. Fat Stacks Blog (FatStacksBlog.com)
5. Quick Sprout (QuickSprout.com)

Pay close attention to how the content is structured on these five sites. Not only do they do a perfect job of teaching the authority site model, they also are perfect examples of bloggers who provide epic content. If you can do the same thing with *your* niche, then you'll have a website that stands out from the competition.

Writing Opportunity #3: Traditional Publishing

Many people dream of landing a contract with a major publishing company. The very idea evokes images of your book being prominently displayed at Barnes & Noble and seeing your name at the top of *The New York Times* Best Seller list. Unfortunately, the reality *rarely* matches this dream.

Over the past decade, the publishing industry has faced a number of setbacks like the growth of Amazon and closures of major book chains (like Borders and Waldenbooks). Circumstances have caused a dramatic decrease in the advances given to new authors. These challenges have made it less advantageous to work with a publishing company.

That said, there are still a few benefits for going the traditional route. Before I dive into the how-to part of this section, let's go over the pros and cons of this business model.

Traditional Publishing Pros

- The publishing company manages the entire process, including editing, or changing the back matter.

- You will receive an advance on the royalties, which can be in the five- to six-figure range *if* you have a proven track record of sales.

- The books will be distributed to major bookstores and select retailers.

- Most of the best-seller lists (like *The New York Times* and *The Wall Street Journal*) rely on sales numbers from a variety of retailers, which are harder to access as a self-published author. This means your chances of hitting these lists are increased if you have the sales to match.

- You will receive some marketing support (but not as much as you would think).

- There are more opportunities to win major book awards, which are important for many genres including literary fiction.

Traditional Publishing Cons

- You typically wait 6-24 months before your book is published after it's picked up by a publishing company.

- Generally you have to find an agent and wait for her to strike a deal with a publishing company, which is not an easy or quick process.

- You get only a fraction of the royalty payment. Sometimes it's as low as 10 to 20 percent of the purchase price.

- You have little control over many book decisions like pricing, cover design, and various promotional campaigns.

- You don't get a lot of marketing support. Often a publisher will leave it up to the authors to market and promote their books. They tend to put their marketing might behind books by authors with a proven track record.

- You also have to go through multiple approvals to make even a small change to the content, like fixing typos.

- Your books directly compete against self-published books, which are typically priced lower.

- You give up rights to your book for set period of time and can't publish it anywhere else, even if the publisher has no intention of exercising the right to create an audiobook, for example.

As I said before, I'm biased when it comes to favoring self-publishing over traditional publishing. That's because I've talked to dozens of authors who went the traditional route and most were unhappy with their contract and the results. But I've also talked to a few authors who enjoy working with a company that guides them through the entire publishing process. So if this sounds like a business model you would like to try, then here is a ten-step process for getting started:

Step #1. Write the Book

If an agent is interested in your book (see below), the first thing she will want to see is the *full manuscript*. So, obviously, you will need to write your book before continuing with this process. Just follow the strategies listed in Chapter Four if you haven't written a book.

Step #2: Buy (or Download) Writer's Market

The best resource for finding an agent for your book is *Writer's Market 2016: The Most Trusted Guide to Getting Published*. (They print a new edition every year, so if you're reading this in 2017 or beyond, then simply look for the most current year.)

Writer's Market is a massive guide that walks you through the process of publishing your work. It includes items like:

- The contact information for thousands of agents and editors.
- Consumer magazine contact information broken down by category and focus.
- Trade journal contact information broken down by industry.
- Lists of writing specific awards and contests.

- Tips on manuscript formatting, writing query letters, building relationships, and how to turn your writing into a full-time business.

The purchase of *Writer's Market Deluxe* comes with a yearlong subscription to a searchable databases for all industry-specific writing categories. So you can easily identify and contact the publishing companies that specialize in your genre or niche.

Since the *Writer's Market* physical book *does not* delve deeply into some markets (for example poetry, short stories, and children's books), I recommend buying the deluxe edition since it will provide you with the largest list of businesses to contact.

Overall, you will quickly discover that *Writer's Market* will become your go-to resource for the contact information of potential agents and publishers. This information is important when you're shopping your book to different agents. So let's talk about that next.

Step #3: Find an Agent

Using *Writer's Market* and the Publisher's Marketplace website (publishersmarketplace.com), create a spreadsheet of agents that specialize in your genre or niche. Be sure to mix in the agents who work with the "big five" companies, mid-level publishers, and independent boutique publishers.

- Include the following on this spreadsheet:
- Name of the agent
- Genre or specialization
- Preferred contact information
- Social media handle(s)
- Any reviews related to authors working with this person
- Any particular information you would like to include in your query letter

You might be tempted to send a mass email to every agent in your genre, but it's better to take your time and be deliberate with your outreach. Remember, these people get dozens—even hundreds—of unsolicited emails every day. So the quickest way to be ignored is to send an unsolicited manuscript that doesn't follow their submission guidelines or isn't a good fit for their niche.

Also, don't send your book to an agent unless she asks for it. Break this rule, and your book will probably be thrown into the slush pile. Instead, start with a query letter to see if the agent might be interested in your manuscript. Let's talk about how to craft this introductory message.

Step #4: Write the Query Letter.

The query letter is a key step to landing a publishing deal. It's a short elevator pitch for your story or nonfiction idea that's similar to the "logline" concept we discussed in Chapter Seven.

A query letter isn't that hard to write. In fact, it's a short message that focuses on eight key points.

- Follow the rules. Most smart agents have a detailed list of how they prefer query letters. Paying attention to these rules shows that you can follow directions and pay attention to the small details. Both will increase your chances of getting to the next hurdle.

- Treat this like a business letter with the agent's name and address at the top. Include your address and phone number as well.

- Address the agent by her name and explain why she is a perfect fit for the book. Mention previous work in this market, titles she's worked on, or something she said on social media.

- Introduce your book with a few basic facts: Working title, total number of words, and the genre. This will provide the agent with a shorthand for what to expect.

- Sell your work by crafting a two- to three-sentence premise. For fiction, include the character, setting, and main problem. For nonfiction, share the audience for the book and the problem you solve or information you provide. Make each word count and don't waste the agent's time with too much description.

- Credits and accolades are important for selling your book. These should include literary awards, editorial reviews you've received from popular figures in your industry, or specific qualifications you have for writing this book.

- For instance, if you are writing a book on diet and weight loss, then you could mention that you are a doctor with 20 years' experience in the areas of nutrition, health, and wellness.

- Talk about your current author platform. If you have a blog with 40,000 monthly readers, 12,000 email subscribers, and 30,000 Facebook fans, then you have an audience that would be interested in your book. To an agent, a large platform means you have a competitive advantage over authors who have little to no presence in a market.

- Keep the query letter to under a page. It should be around four paragraphs: I. Introduction and why you're contacting the specific agent. II. The story pitch. III. Selling information about yourself and your platform. IV. Closing information and how to contact you.

Take your time crafting this query letter. It can make or break your success as an author. Keep tweaking your words until they perfectly contain the essence of your book and demonstrate why it's a good fit for the agent you're addressing.

Step #5: Keep Submitting Your Work.

Expect to be rejected *many* times. Sure it stings. But understand that these rejections are a normal part of the publishing process. Consider this: many agents turned down Stephen King's *Carrie* manuscript before it was published, and J. K. Rowling racked up multiple rejection letters before landing a deal for *Harry Potter and the Sorcerer's Stone*. It happens to all of us, so the best thing you can do is to keep sending those letters out!

Now, what should you do if everyone rejects you?

There can be many reasons why you're being turned down. Perhaps your book (or even the premise) is not that good. But often, rejection happens when the gatekeepers simply don't believe there is a market for your content. If you think this is the case, then self-publishing might be your only shot to get it to the masses. (I'll show you how this process works in the next section.)

Step #6: Send the Full Manuscript

Most agents won't represent a writer until they've read the full manuscript. So the first positive response you'll get is a request to send your book. Some agents want to see only a portion of the manuscript, while others will want the whole thing.

Sometimes an agent will ask for an exclusive read before they agree to read a manuscript. This means you can't send it to anyone else until you get a definitive yes or no answer back from an agent, which can take up to two months.

Choosing to offer an exclusive read is not an easy decision. On one hand, it could lead to a great publishing deal if the agent likes your book and can find a publisher for it. But it also means you're playing the waiting game and not shopping your book to anyone else.

I recommend that you choose exclusivity on a case-by-case basis. If you think it could lead to a great deal, then it's worth doing, but make sure you agree to a small window of time, like two to four weeks. That way, you won't lose too much time if the agent decides to pass on your book.

I'll admit this step can be a tough slog. Typically you would send the manuscript to lots of people and not hear back from most of them. But soon, if you are persistent and have a good book, an agent will contact you to talk more about your project.

Step #7: Meet with Your Prospective Agent

The phone call with a prospective agent is a big deal. This means she sees potential in your work, which *could* result in a publishing deal. You're being screened as a potential client. So it's important to treat this conversation like a job interview.

You should do six things to prepare for this conversation:

1. Review your manuscript and prepare for any questions related to the content.

2. Research the publishing process to understand how advances work and the standard percentage that agents receive.

3. Have a plan, with specific loglines, for any future books you plan to write.

4. Be passionate and professional about your book topic.

5. Think of questions to ask if you're confused about any aspect of the conversation. (It's okay to not know everything about the publishing industry.)

6. Be sure to prepare a thank you note to send after completing the conversation.

At the end of the call (or a few days later) the agent will make a decision. Either she will choose to represent you or she will pass on your book. Most agents will respond promptly, but if you don't hear anything, then it's okay to follow up and ask about her decision.

When you finally strike a deal with an agent, then you'll move on to yet another lengthy step in the process: shopping your book to different publishing companies.

Step #8: Play the Waiting Game

Once the book is in your agent's hands, she will pitch it to different publishing companies. This can be a frustrating period of time because you've done all the hard work and now the process is out of your hands. But there are *two* types of activities that can keep you busy during this period:

First, an agent might ask for a revision of your manuscript. They may ask you to change a plot point, remove huge pieces of text, or even rewrite entire sections. These changes may hurt, but you also have to trust that your agent understands what publishers want from your book.

And then start working on your next book. Remember that even when you have an agent, landing a publishing deal isn't a sure thing. If nobody nibbles on your first book, then it's smart to have another on hand that she can pitch to the publishing companies.

Step #9: Land Your Book Deal!

Hopefully your book will be selected by a publishing house. Their decision depends on a number of factors, which are often out of your control, like reader demand for the genre, the revenue from similar books, and how the company feels about the future of this market. One year vampire romance novels might be in demand, and in the next year, no publishing house will be interested in this genre because readers simply aren't buying.

If things go well, then your agent will eventually land a publishing deal. This is an exciting time, but it's the beginning of another time-consuming part of the process.

Step #10: Working with a Publisher

It takes anywhere from 6-24 months to publish a book. How long it takes to get a book to market depends on your publisher's schedule, the market, and other factors. If they have a large number of book launches lined up for the next year, then you'll have to wait until the calendar clears up before your book goes live.

There are three things that happen during the publishing process:

First, you will work with a professional editor. Yes, you've already edited the book to please your agent, but the goal of this revision is to please *the readers*.

An editor will provide detailed notes of suggested changes. Technically, you can refuse these recommendations, but most of the time, they will vastly improve the quality of the book. So you should follow their advice unless you feel a change will ruin a major part of the narrative.

Second, you might be connected with a publicist. If you're lucky, your publishing house will have a detailed marketing plan, which can include scheduling interviews, landing editorial reviews, and submitting your book for literary awards.

Unfortunately this is the best-case scenario. If your goal is to become a best-selling author or get on *The New York Times* Best Seller list, then it's up to you to create your own success. For your best chance at success, I suggest that you build and leverage your author platform and don't rely solely on the publisher to get your book into the hands of readers. I'll cover how to do that in the final chapter of this book.

The final part of the process is the book launch. While you can cross your fingers and hope for the best, there are many factors that are out of your control when it comes to promoting a book that's been traditionally published. Even if you work hard, a book's success is often predicated on *when* it's released, *who* sees it, and *how* it gets attention in the crowded marketplace.

As you can see, the traditional publishing process is both time consuming and leaves many important decisions to people other than the author. It also involves a lot of hoping and waiting. If you want to control your success, then you might be interested in the perfect business model for writers: self-publishing.

Writing Opportunity #4: Self-Publishing

In my opinion, self-publishing is *the* best way to generate income from your writing. It's not an easy process. But it's a rewarding feeling to work hard on a book, publish it, and see an immediate increase in your income.

Self-publishing differs from the traditional process in a number of ways. For instance, you:

- Avoid having to find an agent or seek permission to publish your content.

- Connect directly with readers without worrying about the gatekeepers.

- Keep a larger percent of the royalties, as high as 70 percent on most book retailer websites.

- Control all aspects of the process including marketing, editing, and cover design.

- Maintain 100 percent control of your book rights and how they're distributed.

- Publish as much (or as little) as you want. You don't have to follow a strict publishing calendar like you might with a publishing house.

Now, I'll admit this model isn't for everyone. As an indie author, the responsibility for every decision falls on your shoulders. It's your job to hire an editor, formatter, and cover designer. You're also responsible for promoting your work and building an author platform. Add these activities to your daily writing habit, and you'll end up juggling a lot of balls.

The good news is self-publishing isn't as hard as you might think. You can find support for every step in the process: all you need to do is hire the right person to handle it.

In this section, I will briefly walk you through the self-publishing business model to show you how it's possible to sell your content directly to an audience without feeling overwhelmed by the entire process.

Step #1: Write Your Book

I've already shown you the steps for how to turn your idea into a book. Suffice it to say, the advice for writing is the same as before: Pick a niche (or genre), find a good logline for that market, write on a daily basis, and then polish the content through multiple drafts.

As you've learned, it's not hard to write a book. The trick is to work on it daily. Remember, even 500 words a day can quickly add up to 15,000 words in a month and 45,000 every quarter. Simply make the commitment to consistency, and you'll have a completed manuscript before you know it.

Step #2: Hire Professional Talent

One of the biggest challenges in self-publishing is thinking that you have to do everything on your own. Fortunately, that's not the case. If you hire quality people to handle each aspect outside your expertise, then you're only responsibility is to write a great book and promote it to your audience.

There are three types of freelancers you should hire for your author business:

1. Cover designer

2. Editor

3. Book formatter

The trick here is knowing *how* to find the right freelancer for each of these tasks. That's why I recommend the following:

- *Hire based on talent.* In other words, don't pick someone just because she charges the least amount of money. Remember that old adage, "You get what you pay for."

- *Examine the freelancer's portfolio.* Ask for and look at their previous projects and evaluate the overall quality. Also, be sure to ask for references from past clients.

- *Contact previous clients.* Email or call former clients to get feedback about the quality of the freelancer's work. You'd be surprised at how often a client wasn't happy with a service but didn't leave a negative review because he didn't want the hassle of dealing with an angry person. You can learn the truth about what it's like to work with this freelancer by having a quick conversation.

- *Email a few questions to the freelancer.* Provide them with the basics about your book and ask if they are comfortable working on it.

What you ask doesn't really matter here. You want to gauge the freelancer's communication style and overall responsiveness. Did you get an immediate response? Does the freelancer understand what's needed? How is their overall attitude toward the project?

You can learn a lot about a freelancer by seeing how they initially interact with you as a potential client.

- *Hire the freelancer.* Your selection should be based on four factors: 1. Quality of previous work. 2. Experience in your genre or market. 3. Responsiveness to your initial queries. 4. What you can afford.

I'll admit that finding three freelancers might sound like a lot of work. But when you get this right, you will have a reliable team member you can turn to whenever you have a new book project. So *where* do you find these superstars? Well, here are seven websites that I recommend:

1. Archangel Ink (getbookhelp.com) is an all-in-one service that I use for many books. Typically, they perform a number of services for my completed manuscript: editing, formatting, print formatting, cover design, and audiobook production. The benefit of going with Archangel is you can pay for a complete book-publishing service or simply get help with one aspect of the process.

2. 99Designs (99designs.com) is a service where you post a design project, like your book cover, and dozens of freelancers submit mock-up examples. You then select finalists based on the submissions and choose the winner to work with you to create a finalized version. 99Designs can be pricey, but it's a great option if you want a professional cover design for your book.

3. Leslie Watts (LeslieWattsEditor.com) offers a variety of editing services you can use to create a polished final draft.

4. KBoards.com is one of the largest forums on indie publishing. If you need help with any self-publishing service, you can reach out to the members and get referrals of freelancers who have previously worked in your genre or niche.

5. Upwork (Upwork.com) is one the largest websites for hiring freelance talent. If you want to find the largest pool of people, then this is a great place to look.

6. Reedsy (Reedsy.com) offers a boutique experience for editing and cover design. Most freelancers here have worked in the publishing industry, so they have a thorough understanding of what will work for your books. But you should also expect to pay more for the freelancers you find here.

7. 3Cs Books (3CsBooks.com) formatted this book and as you can see, is very well done.

These are just seven places where you can get help for your next project. But if you're struggling with finding the right person, then a simple solution is to find a book in your market that you like and ask for a referral from the author. You would be surprised at how often writers are willing to help one another. Most are more than willing to share the name of their favorite editor, formatter, or cover designer.

Step #3: Publish Your Book

There are several online retailers and platforms where you can self-publish your book, but in reality, there are only a handful of sites where you'll make any money. And the king of them all is Amazon.com, which means you'll have to make a hard choice when you first get started.

You can choose to publish exclusively with Amazon Kindle Direct Publishing (through their KDP Select program) or market your books on multiple platforms. The exclusive KDP Select option might be tempting to new authors, but before you make a decision, you need to understand both the advantages and disadvantages of this program.

The advantages of KDP Select (kdp.amazon.com/select) are:

1. You can make your book free for 5 out of every 90 days. You might be thinking, *What do you mean make my books free? I thought the object was to earn money.* You can gain extra visibility in the crowded Amazon marketplace and generate initial attention for your author platform by putting your book on sale or even giving it away for short periods of time.

2. You could also promote your books through Kindle Countdown Deals, which can be as long as one week every 90

days. The idea here is to run a sale event on your book to generate additional income and increase your readership. A benefit of a $0.99 countdown deal is that you earn a 70 percent royalty instead of the typical 35 percent for titles below $2.99.

NOTE: This is an alternative to the five free days. You can pick only one of these two promotional strategies every 90 days.

You also get access to Amazon Marketing Services, which is paid ad platform where you can promote a book to new readers.

3. Your book becomes part of the Kindle Unlimited (KU) program, which is a subscription model similar to Netflix where subscribers pay a monthly fee and can read as many books as they want. As an author, you're compensated for these borrows based on pages read. If you have a long book, then this payout can be fairly lucrative, but if you have a short book, then you won't earn that much money.

4. You also have access to new promotional opportunities that KDP Select rolls out. Amazon is constantly tweaking the indie author experience. And usually the first people to have access to these new tools are authors with books enrolled in KDP Select.

While there are many advantages to KDP Select, there are also legitimate disadvantages that you should consider before you decide whether to go exclusive with Amazon.

1. You won't get full compensation for your book on a Kindle Unlimited borrow, especially if you have a shorter book. While the KU program is great for getting the attention of new readers, it's nowhere near as a profitable as generating an actual sale.

2. You are locked into a 90-day exclusivity contract with Amazon. This means you can't publish on any other platform, even your own website.

3. You might not be fully serving the needs of your audience. Lots of readers refuse to buy anything from Amazon (or

they simply prefer reading books from iBooks or Kobo), so this means you can't sell your book to these readers during your period of exclusivity.

4. You're putting all your eggs in one basket. Amazon is like any other big company. They often change their rules and make decisions that can have a negative impact on your earnings.

As you can see, there are both good and bad aspects of exclusivity through the KDP Select program. Yes, you lose some control of your books, but in exchange, you can get additional marketing help that can jump-start your readership.

Fortunately, I have a simple rule of thumb that can help you make a decision either way.

If you have already built an audience and you're confident these fans will buy your books, then your best option is to publish on every available platform.

If you don't have an audience, then it's best to choose the exclusively of KDP Select at first and use Amazon's massive marketplace to build up your readership. Once you've established yourself as an author and connected with loyal readers, you can pull your books out of KDP Select and submit them to other book platforms.

Hopefully the above will help you figure out the best option for your books. If you decide to publish on multiple platforms, then I recommend eight websites to get started. Instead of wasting a whole day submitting to a site that generates little-to-no sales, I recommend focusing on the following:

#1. Kindle Direct Publishing (KDP) (kdp.amazon.com)

KDP is the platform you use to publish your book on Amazon. The process is fairly intuitive. All you need ahead of time is a book (in an epub or .mobi format) and a cover image. Then you follow a simple process: upload the book to KDP, write a description, add seven keywords, select a few more options and then hit the publish button. Twelve to twenty-four hours later your book is live on Amazon ready for the world to see!

#2. CreateSpace (CreateSpace.com)

CreateSpace is an Amazon-owned print-on-demand company. The benefit here is you can automatically sync your physical books with your KDP account. So whenever a reader is viewing your book on Amazon, he is given the option to buy either the print or ebook version.

Uploading a book to CreateSpace is trickier than the KDP process. Not only do you need a print-ready format, you also need a cover image that includes a back cover. Obviously, you need to spend money on these things, so if you can't afford the additional cost, then it's okay to skip CreateSpace until you can afford to reinvest the money you make from your book-based business.

#3. iBooks (tinyurl.com/ibookspub)

If Amazon is the largest website for self-published authors, then Apple's iBooks platform is a strong contender for second place. With iBooks, you tap into Apple's massive ecosystem of loyal customers. These are people who *only* buy products through this company—including books. So when you publish through iBooks, you'll reach an audience that often ignores Amazon.

The disadvantage of the iBooks platform is you need an Apple computer to submit your book. So if you're a PC user, then you have two options: Hire a freelancer to submit your books. Or use a book distribution service like Draft2Digital (see below).

Overall, if you decide to publish your books on multiple platforms, then iBooks should be the first place to go.

#4: Kobo (writinglife.kobo.com)

This Canadian platform (which sells to over 160 countries) is widely considered to be the most indie-friendly book publishing service. Not only does Kobo have a growing base of readers, they also work with self-published authors to maximize their sales.

#5. Nook (nookpress.com)

Nook (a company owned by Barnes & Noble) was once a popular website for self-published authors. Unfortunately, they've lost a lot of market share and have been forced to shut down their services to every country besides the United States. There's even a chance that Barnes & Noble will shut down the Nook project altogether.

So, *if* it's still possible to publish to Nook, then it's worth the extra 10 minutes of effort. But if it isn't, then it's okay to skip it.

#6. Draft2Digital (draft2digital.com)

Time management is a skill *all* authors should develop. If your day is filled with administration tasks (like submitting your books to dozens of platforms), then you *won't* have enough time to write. My point? While it's tempting to upload your book directly to every available site, you might be better off focusing on a few (like Amazon, iBooks, and Kobo) then using Draft2Digital (D2D) service to submit your book everywhere else.

Currently with D2D, you can publish to these websites:

- iBooks
- Nook
- Kobo
- Inktera
- Scribd
- Tolino
- 24Symbol

Just to be clear, D2D charges 15 percent of the royalties for the use of their service. Sure, you're losing a little bit of money, but it's worth it because you'll have the convenience of managing your books in a single location (instead of six different places).

#7. Smashwords (SmashWords.com)

Smashwords offers a similar service to D2D. While it's connected to more sites than D2D, Smashwords isn't as user friendly as its competitor. The publishing process is very confusing, and you get paid quarterly instead of monthly. I recommend using Smash-Words *only* to publish to the sites not available through D2D.

#8. Gumroad (GumRoad.com)

The best long-term strategy as a self-published author is to sell your books directly to your fans. The simplest way to do this is through Gumroad. This platform makes it easy to accept payments that you can fully integrate into your website. So if you want to sell direct, then this is a great tool for getting started.

Step #4: Get Started with Self-Publishing

The key to successful self-publishing is to leverage a writer's platform, which is what I'll cover in the next chapter. Beyond that, there is a lot to learn and master if you want to consistently sell your books. If self-publishing is something you'd like to try, then here are my favorite (free) resources where you can learn more about this business model:

Websites

Authority.pub is a website that I own. The goal here is to show you how to build an authority in a niche and publish a series of quality books related to the topic. If you liked the content you found in *The Miracle Morning for Writers*, then you'll love all the information we provide about the self-publishing process on Authority.pub.

- *The Creative Penn* (thecreativepenn.com) is run by Joanna Penn, a successful fiction *and* nonfiction author. In her blog and podcast, she covers every aspect of what it takes to start and run a successful author business.

- Writership has been mentioned a few times in this book. The website is a great resource for learning about the craft of writing and editing your books.

- David Gaughran (davidgaughran.wordpress.com) runs a website with current news and his insightful reflections on the self-publishing industry.

- Jane Friedman's website (janefriedman.com) is full of actionable content and detailed strategies for the aspiring author.

- *The Writer's Café* section on Kboards (kboards.com/index.php/board.60.0.html) is where a lot of smart self-published authors gather. Be sure to check out the most-viewed threads *and* ask questions whenever you're stuck with any step in the process. You'll find lots of insightful threads posted here, so be sure to check it out regularly.

- Mastermind.pub is my publishing-specific Facebook group. With almost 5,000 members, there are lots of great conversations happening on this page.

Podcasts

Listening to podcasts is the best way to fully leverage routine activities where you can't be hands-free, like driving, exercising, or doing chores. Instead of tuning out to music, you can use this time to fill your mind with publishing-related knowledge.

It's not hard to check out podcasts. Simply download the iTunes or Stitcher app to your phone, type the names of the shows listed below in the search bar, and then subscribe to the ones that look interesting. Once subscribed, your phone will get automatic updates whenever a new episode is published.

If you're interested in publishing-related podcast shows, then here are a few that I recommend:

- *Authority Self-Publishing* is the show that I host with my partners Barrie Davenport and Ron Clandenin. In each episode, we cover one aspect of self-publishing and do a deep dive into that topic.

- *Self Publishing Podcast* is the first publishing-related podcasts that I checked out, and it's still one of my favorites. It's hosted by three prolific fiction and nonfiction authors and is chock-full of information about what they're *currently doing* to build their book-based business.

NOTE: This show is *not* safe for work because they curse a lot. I don't feel this takes away from the quality of the content, but it might not be for you if you're offended by certain language.

- *Sell More Books Show*, hosted by Jim Kukral and Bryan Cohen, is a weekly podcast that reviews publishing-related news and tips. If you don't have time to read blogs or forum posts, then this is a great way to stay on top of information you can use to grow your business.

- *Rocking Self-Publishing* focuses on in-depth interviews with successful fiction and nonfiction authors. What I love about this show is that host Simon Whistler asks great questions that force the guests to provide more details instead of only basic answers.

- There is also *The Creative Penn Podcast*, which was previously mentioned in the websites section. Be sure to check it out as well!

Books

There are a *lot* of books on self-publishing, so it's hard to know where to start. I suggest that you check out the books that tackle the specific problems and questions you might have about the publishing process. Here are a few suggestions:

- *Let's Get Digital* by David Gaughran provides a very detailed overview of the self-publishing industry and why it's the best option for almost every writer.

- *Write. Publish. Repeat.* by Sean Platt, Johnny B. Truant, and David Wright is a call-to-arms for consistently writing books and taking control of your author business. They tell the story of their early publishing efforts and offer advice for people who are starting out.

- *Iterate and Optimize* (by the same authors) is a follow-up book that maps out a plan for using your existing content to improve your sales and increase the value of your readership.

- *2K to 10K* by Rachel Aaron details a step-by-step strategy for increasing your word count and what you produce on a daily basis.

- *Take Off Your Pants* by Libbie Hawker discusses the value of plotting (instead of "pantsing") your books. Not only does Hawker make an effective argument for creating in-depth outlines, she shows you how to do it in a step-by-step process.

- *Prosperity for Writers* by our wonderful coauthor Honorée Corder demonstrates how it's possible to create great content and make *real* money from it. Here she debunks the "starving artist" myth, provides specific examples of successful writers who run passion-based businesses that are also profitable, and gives you the steps you can take to become a prosperous writer yourself.

- *Business for Authors* by Joanna Penn is a great starting point for turning your writing into an actual business. In this book, she discusses the financial, legal, and business management decisions you need to make to build a successful author career.

- *Dictate Your Book* by Monica Leonelle explains how narration can become a great way to increase your word count. This is the perfect guide for anyone who wants to "level up" their writing.

There are many more self-publishing resources, but these websites, podcasts, and books can give you a world-class education for under $100. My advice is to completely immerse yourself in this world and learn everything you can about the process. What you'll discover is that, while the concepts are easy to learn, what's important is to go out there and make things happen!

With that in mind, let's move on to the final chapter where I will share a concept that's important no matter what type of business model you select. Whether you're a blogger, freelancer, indie author or you're looking to land a deal with a publishing house, *all* of these options require you to build a writer's platform.

In the next section, I'll give you a step-by-step strategy for getting started.

— 9 —

NOT-SO-OBVIOUS WRITING PRINCIPLE #6:

BUILDING A WRITER PLATFORM

In a popular article Kevin Kelly talked about an important concept called *1,000 True Fans*. The idea is simple: If you have 1,000 loyal fans who buy *everything* you create and pay an average of $100 per year, then you will generate a decent yearly income.

What's attractive about the 1,000 True Fans concept is that you don't need to be super famous or sell millions of books to earn a good income from your writing. All that's required is to find your tribe and create the content that *they* want.

Now, when it comes to writing, it's not easy generate $100 per reader since you're limited by the number of books you can produce each year. But if you change the goal to *10,000* true fans each paying an average of $10, then this number becomes very realistic.

So how do you hit this golden 10,000 true fans milestone?

The short answer is to build a writer platform where you develop a relationship with fans and leverage their love for your content to direct attention to all your writing projects.

You can break down a writer platform into eight components:

1. Build an email list.

2. Pick a content distribution method like a blog, YouTube channel, or podcast.)

3. Create great content on a consistent basis.

4. Leverage one or two social media channels (Facebook, Twitter, Instagram, Pinterest, LinkedIn, or Google Plus).

5. Drive traffic to your books and content platform.

6. Network with authors and authorities in your market.

7. Use your books to build readership.

8. Focus on the activities that get results.

I'll tell you up front… building your writer platform takes time and effort. But don't worry too much about this because if you start small and focus on one component at a time, it's not hard to gain attention in your market while still having the time to write.

This concept is important *even* if you're focusing on building a freelance career. A writer platform not only demonstrates your knowledge and expertise, it's also a great way to attract attention to your service.

So, let's talk about the eight key components for building a writer platform.

Component #1: Start an Email List

Nowadays, when you think of promoting a book, the first strategy people might think of is to hop on social media to share it with their friends and family. The truth is social media *helps*, but it doesn't compare to the results you'll get with an email list. That's because when you rely on other websites to reach your audience, you'll have limited access to directly talk to your audience.

In this chapter, you will discover numerous ideas for building a writer platform. It's okay to skip most of them, but I'd consider email marketing to be a *mandatory step* in the process.

You will need three items to build an email list:

First, you need an email marketing service. This is a tool that's used to maintain the contact information for your readers, which allows you to send messages on a regular basis. This service simplifies the process of contacting your subscribers. It takes just a much time to message 10 people as it does for 10,000 people.

There are three good options when it comes to email marketing:

1. MailChimp (mailchimp.com) lets you open a free account for up to 2,000 subscribers. It's a great option if you're on a limited budget.

The downside of the free account is that you can't create an autoresponder sequence, which is an important aspect of building a writer platform. You want your welcome message(s) to go to the people who sign up for your email list automatically. My suggestion is this: As soon as you can invest money in your business, either pay for a professional account with MailChimp or go with one of the other options listed below.

2. Aweber (aweber.com) is the service that I've used for over a decade, so it's the one I mention whenever someone asks for a recommendation. Aweber uses an intuitive interface for managing your subscribers, and they make it easy to write and send out your messages.

3. Convert Kit (convertkit.com) is an interesting new alternative to the two other services. It has a number of automation tools and can be fully integrated with a number of websites (like Gumroad, WordPress, and Leadpages.)

All three email marketing services are great options. I recommend that you start with MailChimp and then move to Aweber when you can invest more money in your marketing efforts.

The second thing you need to build an email list is a piece of content called a *lead magnet*. Nowadays, people are very cautious about giving out their email addresses. So many writers offer an "ethical bribe" to encourage readers to sign up for their lists. That free offer is often called a lead magnet.

A lead magnet could be a variety of things:

- A short story about one of your main characters
- The first book in your series
- A "quick start" guide of the tactics covered in your book
- A numbered list of tips and strategies
- A collection of links to resources related to your niche
- A detailed, step-by-step walk-through of one strategy

A quality lead magnet should be something that readers *actually* want. A good way to determine the value of this offer is to ask yourself: "Is this something people would pay money to receive?"

If there is legitimate value in your offer, then it would make a great lead magnet.

The final item you need to build an email list is a web page to capture the email addresses of your readers. This is often called a *squeeze page*.

A squeeze page should sync with your email marketing service. Not only should it capture your subscriber's contact information, it should also automatically deliver your lead magnet (usually in the introductory email).

The advantage of a squeeze page (over a regular page on your website) is that you give readers a simple A or B option: either they join your list, or they leave the page. So if you can sell the value of your lead magnet, then you can quickly build an email list of subscribers who like your content. This means you'll have an asset that can be leveraged whenever you have something new to share.

There are three options for creating squeeze pages:

1. Instapage (instapage.com)
2. Optimize Press (optimizepress.com)
3. Lead Pages (leadpages.net)

Another option is to hire a Fiverr gig provider, which typically costs $5 to $10 to build a squeeze page for you. Sometimes the quality isn't the best on Fiverr, but it's a great solution if you need a squeeze page and can't spend that much money on it currently.

Component #2: Pick a Content Platform

Readers want to know the writer behind the books. A great way to strengthen your relationships is to build a content distribution platform. Popular options include a blog, podcast, or You-Tube channel. I call it "content distribution" because you create free information and distribute it to the masses to build an online following.

What *type* of content platform you choose is up to you. Each has its own advantages and disadvantages. Since you're a writer, I'll assume that you naturally gravitate to writing, but you also might want to save your creative juices for books and instead communicate with your audience through videos or a podcast.

If you're unsure about what to pick, then read over the benefits of each platform.

Option #1: Blogging as a Platform

This is the easiest for writers simply because we spend our time writing. This means you won't have to learn a brand new skill to create content.

Another advantage of blogging is you can repurpose content. You can take segments from your book and post them on your site. Or, you can test a book idea first with your blog readers and use their feedback to write your next book. Both strategies are great for leveraging the content you've *already* created to connect with your audience.

The final advantage is you build traffic through search engine optimization. This is a great option for nonfiction writers because people use Google all the time to find information. If your page ranks well for a keyword (and it relates to one of your books), then you can drive a lot of potential readers to your book(s).

Option #2: Podcasting as a Platform

If you're a natural conversationalist, then podcasting is a great way to build up your tribe. The strategy is similar to writing books: you identify a market, create content that focuses on a specific topic, and then publish on a consistent schedule.

There are three advantages to starting a podcast.

First, you build a strong connection with your audience. It's similar to listening to your favorite talk show. You provide value to your audience, and they get to know you better as a person. The relationships you build with listeners is often better than that with blog readers because listeners feel like they know you—even if they've never met you before.

Another benefit is you can leverage a podcast to meet the biggest names in your industry. They get an opportunity to share their product or service with a new audience. And in return, you get an opportunity to introduce yourself to someone who is often too busy to respond to most requests. If your goal is to build your expertise in a market, then a quick way to hack this process is to interview experts in your industry.

Also, chances are the interviewee will share a link to the podcast or mention it to her fans, so you'll gain exposure to a new audience.

The final advantage is you can tap into a built-in audience that already listens to podcasts. Websites like iTunes and Stitcher have millions of users. If you become one of the go-to leaders in your market, then it's possible to get a lot of attention for your show and, more importantly, *more readers* for your books.

Unfortunately, the downside of podcasting is it requires a bit of technological know-how. You have to acquire software, a recording mic, and editing tools. If you're interested in starting a podcast, I suggest that you check out this *free* tutorial: How to

Start a Podcast Tutorial by Pat Flynn (smartpassiveincome.com/how-to-start-a-podcast-podcasting-tutorial/).

Option #3: YouTube as a Platform

YouTube marketing is another way to build up a loyal following. If you can create short, actionable videos that viewers love, then you'll build a stronger connection than what's possible with blogging or podcasting.

There are two advantages of using YouTube as a platform.

First, YouTube is the second largest search engine on the Internet. So there are lots of people using this site to find content. (The site boasts over one billion mobile video views *every day*.) If you're providing quality content in a nonfiction market, then it's not hard to build your platform and get more attention for your books.

The second advantage of YouTube is it's perfect for "demonstration niches." If you can explain your concept with a how-to video, then this might be the platform for you. For example, if you write about technology, fitness, or DIY markets, then you should consider building a YouTube platform.

Video marketing is similar to podcasting because you need to master a few technological challenges. Not only do you need to select the right camera, you should also understand lighting and how to edit the raw video. These skills don't often come naturally to your average writer. So I recommend checking out the free information that James Wedmore provides to learn more about this process (www.jameswedmore.com).

Component #3: Create Epic Content

We've already talked about the importance of creating epic content. This is a phrase that's often repeated, but rarely understood. Epic content isn't about hitting a specific word count or writing a certain type of blog post. It's about knowing what your audience wants and giving it to them on a continual basis.

If you study authorities who create great content, then you'll see they do it in two distinct ways:

Option 1: Detailed, How-To Information

This is the quality over quantity approach where you publish on an infrequent basis. When you *do* release a piece of content, it's usually one of the *best* in that particular market. This helps you build an audience because you become a person who is known for creating high-level content.

As an example, think back to the podcasting tutorial that I mentioned before. This tutorial was created by Pat Flynn, one of the top online business authorities around.

Pat's video tutorial teaches you everything you need to know about the podcasting process. Not only does he demonstrate the sound quality of different mics, he also shows you how to record an episode and upload it to different podcasting platforms.

The interesting thing is Pat offers these lessons as a *free* tutorial. Sure, he earns money through a few affiliate commission links, but these lessons are better than most of the paid courses available on the market.

My final point here is that Pat has a long history of providing top-level content to his audience. So when he launched *Will It Fly* in January 2016, his followers were there to buy the book and leave glowing reviews. Because Pat provides great content on a continual basis, he was able to leverage his relationship with his audience and land his book on *The Wall Street Journal Best Selling Books* list.

Option 2: Regular, Bite-Sized Content

Another way to build an audience is to publish consistent content. Usually each article (or episode) is short, but the cumulative effect of the information builds a loyal brand because followers will get detailed explanations for many challenges related to that niche.

The best example of this principle can be found with Mignon Fogarty's Grammar Girl (quickanddirtytips.com/grammar-girl) brand. Her podcast episodes aren't very long, but each one focuses on answering one writing question. Listeners love this show because it's entertaining *and* full of great information.

You shouldn't feel like you need to pick one strategy over the other. Perhaps you could build an audience with short articles and occasionally sprinkle in a super-sized blog post. The important thing to remember is to be consistent and look for ways to best serve your audience.

Component #4: Build a Social Media Presence

Like it or not, social media is part of the current business experience. I've noticed that most writers have a love-hate relationship with social media. Sure it's a great tool for connecting with readers, but it also requires a time investment that can get in the way of writing.

There is a common misconception that you need to be on *all* social media platforms. Actually, it's more effective to focus on just one or two and build momentum by consistently publishing quality updates. To find the right platforms for you, check out a few thoughts on the more popular sites:

- Facebook (facebook.com) is the most popular social site, but recent changes to its algorithm have diminished the reach you can expect from your fan page. This means you have to invest money in their ad platform in order to grow your audience.

An alternative strategy to building a fan page is to participate in Facebook groups. If you join a group related to your niche (and add value to the members), then you can get attention for your platform. This is a great strategy for any writer who is just getting started and doesn't have an existing fan base.

- Twitter (twitter.com) has often been described as the ultimate cocktail party. Here you can jump into conversations and add value to what's being discussed. But as with any in-person event, it's important to make a good first impression. You shouldn't initiate a conversation and immediately pitch one of your books. Instead, add value by answering questions and sharing good resources that you don't own.

Another advantage of Twitter is its surprisingly easy to reach celebrities and experts in your niche. You might not get a response to every Tweet, but if you consistently add value, then you increase the chance of getting their attention, which could be parlayed into an interview for your next book, podcast, or blog post.

- LinkedIn (LinkedIn.com) is a great social site if you create business-focused content. Not only can you connect with other professionals, but this platform also has groups where you can interact with others, share your thoughts, and occasionally link to your content.

- I've lumped Instagram (instagram.com) and Pinterest (pinterest.com) together because they will work only for certain markets. If you are in a visual niche or you can incorporate eye-catching images related to your topic, then there are a lot of potential readers on these sites. I suggest that you join each site, observe what other successful authors in your niche are doing, and then look for strategies that can be applied to your writing business.

- Blab (blab.me), Periscope (periscope.tv), and Facebook Live (live.fb.com) are all part of the new wave of technology to live-stream videos directly to your audience. The benefit of these platforms is they're brand new, so it'll will be easier to gain traction because they haven't been saturated with too many marketers. So if you are a natural conversationalist, then you might want to try one of these sites.

These are just a few of the more popular social media platforms. Some might be great for growing your brand, while others would be a complete waste of time. I recommend that you pick one or two, provide consistent value, and then see if this effort has a positive impact on your platform after a few months.

A word of warning: it's easy to spend too much time on social media. That's why I recommend installing the Rescue Time (RescueTime.com) program, which tracks your computer time and provides you with a daily and weekly report of where you spend the most time.

With Rescue Time, you will have hard data so you know if you're focusing on important activities (like writing) or if you're wasting hours checking Facebook. If you're worried about not being able to focus on your author business, then I recommend installing this tool on your computer.

Component #5: Drive Traffic to Your Platform

It's important to drive web traffic to your platform, not just to Amazon, iBooks, or Kobo. Yes, these sites are great for making money, but they also change their rules anytime they want. If potential readers aren't visiting your website, then you're one rule change away from failure.

The best traffic generation strategy is to provide helpful information on your website then promote your lead magnet within the content. Then all you have to do is publish great information on a regular basis to grow your audience and promote it through the different traffic channels (like Facebook, Twitter, etc.) And finally, once you've built up an email list, you can promote your books (or other offers). The strategy looks like this:

Traffic source where readers gather —> send them to your site by answering a question or providing a resource —> offer lead magnet, which gets them to join your list —> provide more great content and promote your books.

Remember, your goal is to provide value to the reader and then continue to add more value through your lead magnet or email list. Once the subscriber knows you better, you can offer your book as something they would enjoy reading or find helpful. Sounds easy, right?

Now this strategy doesn't work only for nonfiction writers. Fiction authors can do this too.

Let's say you write horror stories. You could create a post with the scariest novels ever written, like *The Shining*, *Haunting of Hill House*, *The Exorcist*, and *Ghost Story*. Then at the end of the article, you could include a squeeze page that promotes a free copy of your horror story. Odds are, since the people reading this page are interested in horror, they will join your list to check out your story.

There are countless ways to send traffic to a website, but here are nine ideas that work best for a writer's platform.

1. Build readership on WattPad (WattPad.com) by posting installments of your fiction.

2. Write quality articles and blog posts related to your market on Medium (Medium.com).

3. Answer niche-specific questions on Quora (Quora.com).

4. Use Google's Keyword Planner (adwords.google.com/KeywordPlanner) tool to identify keywords related to your niche and write articles on your site for that market.

5. Build connections with readers on Goodreads (goodreads.com).

6. Network with popular authorities in your niche and write high-value guest posts on their sites.

7. Do podcast interviews and provide helpful content to the audience.

8. Run Facebook Ads (facebook.com/business/products/ads) to your target audience with links to high-value content or your email list.

9. Turn your content into SlideShare (slideshare.net) presentations.

Generating web traffic should be a top priority for your writer platform. You don't need to be everywhere to build an audience. In fact, if you can master only a few of the nine ideas I just listed, then it's possible to get plenty of attention from your ideal readers.

Component #6: Leverage Your Books

When you publish a book, it's important to turn the casual reader into a raving fan.

A perfect example of this is Hal Elrod, the coauthor of this book. Not only does *The Miracle Morning* provide a step-by-step strategy that readers can use to improve their lives, it also includes plenty of opportunities for true fans to reach out to him and join the community that he's built.

If you look closely at how *The Miracle Morning* is structured, you'll see that he includes links to his Facebook group, email list, and free content that he's created.

This is a great strategy that *you* should implement as an author. Never assume that a reader knows how to find you. Your job is to provide an easy way to contact you and learn more about your offerings. This can be done by linking to some (or all) of the following in your books:

- A lead magnet with bonus content related to the topic
- Blog posts, podcast episodes, or YouTube videos that you've created
- A Facebook group where readers can interact with one another
- Your social media profiles
- Email address or other contact information
- A resources section that includes hyperlinks mentioned in the book.

Simply consider what would add the most value and then include it your book. Not only does this improve the reader's experience, it also helps them take that next step toward becoming a true fan.

Component #7: Network with Other Authors and Authorities

Networking is important for writers because you can build strategic alliances to help each other with critical projects. The key here is to *not* keep score about who owes whom. Instead, form a friendship (over a period of time) where you learn to rely on one another when you need help.

If you're looking to network with other content creators, then the best place to look are Facebook groups and forums.

One option is to join groups associated to your niche. Type in a keyword phrase in the Facebook search bar and join the active groups that you find. And if you're looking for a forum, simply enter the keyword and "forum" into Google to find the best sites (e.g., personal finance forum).

You could also network with writers who create content around a variety of topics. Here are a number of suggestions for where to go:

Facebook Groups

- The Miracle Morning Community

  (facebook.com/groups/MyTMMCommunity/)

- Pat Flynn's Self-Publishing Group

  (facebook.com/groups/357112331027292/)

- Prosperity for Writers

  (facebook.com/groups/ProsperityforWriters)

- The Write Life Community

  (facebook.com/groups/TheWriteLifeGroup/)

- Blogging Boost

  (facebook.com/groups/bloggingboost/)

Forums

- Writer's Café on KBoards

  (kboards.com/index.php/board.60.0.html)

- Goodreads Groups

  (goodreads.com/group)

- Writing Forums

  (writingforums.org)

- Absolute Write

  (absolutewrite.com/forums)

Similar to the other strategies mentioned in this book, your goal with networking is to be a helpful member of the community *before* asking for anything in return. Build strategic alliances so that people see you as a trusted expert before promoting anything.

Here are four ideas for growing your network of contacts:

1. Be an awesome, helpful person. Don't let the word "help" scare you. Sometimes all a member needs is an in-depth answer to a specific question. Other ways you can help include sharing someone's content on social media, buying their book, leaving a review, or simply be an evangelist for their brand.

Keep a short list of your online friends and stay on top of their projects. Whenever they promote something that's personally important, look for an opportunity to help out.

2. Think quality over quantity. It takes time to build a network, so don't try to rush the process. In fact, it's better to focus on a handful of quality relationships instead of trying to meet hundreds of people. It's usually these strong relationships that will provide the most help for your next important writing project.

3. Ask for help (for important projects). Don't be afraid to reach out whenever you need assistance with an important project. But do this only when you *truly* need help. There is a fine line between leveraging your relationships and being that mooch who's always asking for favors.

4. Create strategic alliances. This is an advanced networking strategy where you join forces and work on a project that positively impacts both of your businesses. An alliance could mean a number of things including the following:

- Join a genre-specific, multi-author book event
- Speak at an online summit
- Collaborate on a book.
- Participate in a roundup post that answers a simple question
- Submit a guest post to a popular website
- Request an interview for your blog or podcast

It's impossible to build any type of business in isolation. In fact, the best way to grow your platform is to interact with people who share a similar passion for your market. Sure, there often isn't an immediate value exchange for building these relationships. But you'll find that over the months—and even years—there will be plenty of opportunities where you can help one another out.

Component #8: Focus on Your 80-20 Activities

The 80-20 rule has been my guiding business principle for over a decade. Italian economist Vilfredo Pareto discovered the principle that 80 percent of your results typically come from 20 percent of your effort.

This rule can be applied to *any* industry or business. Eighty percent of revenue is generated by the 20 percent of the salespeople. Eighty percent of complaints come from only 20 percent of customers. And 80 percent of highway traffic is funneled through 20 percent of the roads.

My point here is that, no matter what you do with your writing business, there will *always* be actions that produce extraordinary results. So a few strategies will work well while everything else will be a waste of your time.

Why is it important to focus on the 80-20 rule?

The answer is simple: When you focus on the strategies that actually work (and eliminate everything else), you will have a competitive advantage over the writers who try to do a dozen things every day.

For instance, let's say you want to gain attention for your platform, so you try every strategy mentioned in *The Miracle Morning for Writers*. You would need to write books, upload them to Amazon, upload them to other platforms, create blog content, record podcast episodes, upload videos to YouTube, write articles on Medium, answer questions on Quora, interact in multiple Facebook groups, post Twitter updates, snap photos for Instagram, design eye-catching images for Pinterest, answer email, create information products, and record audiobooks.

Sounds exhausting, doesn't it?

While I've included lots of strategies in this book, this doesn't mean you should try them all. In fact, it's smarter to focus on a few, see what works, and then eliminate everything else.

To put this idea into action, I recommend doing the following on a monthly basis:

- Analyze the traffic coming your website. Install Google Analytics (google.com/analytics) to get this information.

- Identify which content you've created gets the most views and shares.

- Find out what generates the most email subscribers.

- Track your royalties on the various book platforms to see what generates the best income.

- Track your royalties on a per-book basis to see which content resonates the best with your audience.

- Identify the clients who generate the highest return on your time.

- Identify the clients who cause the most headaches and hassles.

When you do an 80-20 analysis, you'll discover that only a handful of activities or people produce the best results for your business. Often you will discover that the biggest challenges in your business are caused by one or two bottlenecks. Once you've conducted this 80-20 analysis, try to focus on the "big win" activities to the exclusion of everything else.

For instance, I focus on only a few strategies to grow my platform including:

- Writing books and blog content

- Recording episodes and interviewing experts for my podcast

- Creating videos and content for my course

- Interacting in a *few* Facebook groups

- Answering emails from readers and folks in my network

- Meeting with my business partners and planning future strategies

- Managing my virtual team and helping them coordinate important routine activities

These activities are a pretty good mix—half of my time is spent on content creation and half on marketing and networking. If you paid close attention here, you would notice two things:

1. I don't do a number of administrative tasks because I've created a process for each one and trust in the people I've hired to manage the process.

2. I ignore many activities that are recommended by many online marketing experts. This is not because I think they're bad ideas, but because I have found that they don't work for *my* business.

The lesson I want you to learn here is you have only a limited time for writing. It's not something that can be delegated or outsourced. This means that you need to be more careful with your time than other entrepreneurs.

So instead of spinning your wheels and trying to do a dozen things, take the time to figure out what works for *your* business and then eliminate everything else, even if that means saying "no" to 9 out of 10 opportunities that come across your desk. Only then can you take your writing business to the next level.

Congratulations! You've learned everything you need to know to build a writing-focused daily routine. Now you can start your day with the Miracle Morning and then schedule time to focus on building a writing business that connects with your passion and generates a steady income. Moreover, you'll never have to worry about writer's block again because you'll have the tools and process in place to continuously come up with great book ideas. Finally, you know how to build a writer platform that will help you get attention in a crowded marketplace and find those true fans who can support your work.

Before you go, there's one more piece for you to add to your arsenal, the Miracle Equation. Are you ready? Turn the page …

THE MIRACLE EQUATION

BY HAL ELROD

It's time to take everything you've learned so far and bring it together with the ultimate success equation that ALL top achievers—in every field—use to consistently produce extraordinary results.

You know now that you can wake up early, maintain extraordinary levels of energy, direct your focus, and master the not-so-obvious writing skills. But I know you didn't read this far merely to take your success up a notch. You want to make quantum leaps and generate extraordinary results, right? Right. If you also apply what follows to your writing career, you're going to go much further: you're going to join the successful authors—*the top one percent.*

To make those leaps, there is one more crucial strategy that you must add to your writer's toolbox, and it's called the Miracle Equation.

The Miracle Equation is the underlying strategy that I used to consistently break sales records, become one of the youngest individuals ever inducted into my company's hall of fame, and go on to become a number one bestselling author and international keynote speaker. But it's more than that. It is precisely the same equation that ALL top performers—that top one percent—have used to create awe-inspiring results, while the other 99 percent wonder how they do it.

The Miracle Equation was born during one of my Cutco push periods, a 14-day span during which the company fostered friendly competition and created incentives to bring in record sales, both for the salesperson and the office.

This particular push period was special for two reasons. First, I was trying to become the first sales representative in company history to take the number one spot for three consecutive push periods. Second, I'd have to do it while being able to work only 10 of the 14 days.

I knew I needed to dig deep to achieve such a feat and that fear and self-doubt were a much greater hurdle than usual. In fact, I considered lowering my sales goal based on the circumstances. Then I remembered what one of my mentors, Dan Casetta, had taught me: "The purpose of a goal isn't to hit the goal. The real purpose is to develop yourself into the type of person who can achieve your goals, regardless of whether you hit that particular one or not. It is who you become by giving it everything you have until the last moment—regardless of your results—that matters most."

I made a decision to stick with my original goal, even though the possibility of failing to achieve it was a real risk based on the limited time frame. With only ten days to set a record, I knew I needed to be especially focused, faithful, and intentional. It was an ambitious objective, no question, and as you'll see, one that required me to find out what I was really made of!

Two Decisions

As with any great challenge, I needed to make decisions related to achieving the goal. I reverse-engineered the push period by asking myself, "If I were to break the record in just ten days, what decisions would I have to make and commit to in advance?"

I identified the two that would make the biggest impact. Only later did I realize that these were *the same two decisions that all top-performers make at some point in their careers.*

Those two decisions became the basis for The Miracle Equation.

The First Decision: Unwavering Faith

Knowing that I was already facing fear and self-doubt, I realized that to achieve the seemingly impossible, I would have to decide to maintain unwavering faith each and every day, *regardless of my results.* I knew that there would be moments when I would doubt myself and times when I would be so far off track that the goal would no longer seem achievable. But it would be those moments when I would have to override self-doubt with unshakeable faith.

To keep that level of faith in those challenging moments, I repeated what I call my Miracle Mantra:

I will _____ (make the next sale, call 20 prospects, reach my goal), no matter what. There is no other option.

Understand that maintaining unwavering faith isn't *normal.* It's not what most people do. When it doesn't look like the desired result is likely, average performers give up the faith that it's possible. When the game is on the line, a team is down on the scorecards, and there are only seconds left, it is only the elite performers—the Michael Jordans of the world—who, without hesitation, tell their team, "Give me the ball."

The rest of the team breathes a sigh of relief because of their fear of missing the game-winning shot, while Michael Jordan made a decision at some point in his life that he would maintain unwavering faith, despite the fact that he might miss. (And although Michael Jordan missed 26 game-winning shots in his career, his faith that he would make every single one never wavered.)

That's the first decision that the world's elite make, and it's yours for the making, too.

When you're working toward a goal and you're not on track, what is the first thing that goes out the window? The faith that the outcome you want so much is possible. Your self-talk becomes *I'm not on track. It doesn't look like I'm going to reach my goal.* And with each passing moment, your faith decreases.

You don't have to settle for that. You have the ability and the choice to maintain that same unwavering faith, no matter what, and regardless of the results. You may sometimes doubt yourself or have a bad day, but you must find—and re-find—your faith that all things are possible and hold it throughout your journey, whether it is a 10-day push period or a 30-year career.

Elite athletes maintain unwavering faith that they can make every shot they take. That faith—and the faith you need to develop—isn't based on probability. It draws from a whole different place. Most salespeople operate based on what is known as the law of averages. But what we're talking about here is the law of miracles. When you miss shot after shot—in your case, sale after sale—you have to tell yourself what Michael Jordan tells himself, I've missed three, but I want the ball next, and I'm going to make that next shot.

And if you miss that one, your faith doesn't waiver. You repeat the Miracle Mantra to yourself:

I will _____ (write 1,000 words, jot down five ideas for my next book, reach my goal), no matter what. There is no other option.

Then, you simply uphold your integrity and do what it is that you say you are going to do.

An elite athlete may be having the worst game ever, where it seems like in the first three-quarters of the game, they can't make a shot to save their life. Yet in the fourth quarter, right when the team needs them, they start making those shots. They always want the ball; they always have belief and faith in themselves. In the fourth quarter, they score three times as many shots as they've made in the first three-quarters of the game.

Why? They have conditioned themselves to have unwavering faith in their talents, skills, and abilities, regardless of what it says on the scoreboard or their stats sheet.

And …

They combine their unwavering faith with part two of The Miracle Equation: extraordinary effort.

The Second Decision: Extraordinary Effort

When you allow your faith to go out the window, effort almost always follows right behind it. *After all*, you tell yourself, *what's the point in even trying to write a book or achieve your goal if it's not possible?* Suddenly, you find yourself wondering how you're ever going to find the next new marketer or sell another product, let alone reach the big goal you've been working toward.

I've been there many times, feeling deflated, thinking, *what's the point of even trying?* As a writer, if you're halfway through a month and you should have written 15,000 words but you're only at 10,000, you begin to think, *There's no way I can make it.*

That's where extraordinary effort comes into play. You need to stay focused on your original goal—you need to connect to the vision you had for it, that big why you had in your heart and mind when you set the goal in the first place.

Like me, you need to reverse engineer the goal. Ask yourself, *If I'm at the end of this month and this goal were to have happened, what would I have done? What would I have needed to do?*

Whatever the answer, you will need to take massive action and give it everything you have, regardless of your results. You have to believe you can still ring the bell of success at the end. You have to maintain unwavering faith and extraordinary effort—until the buzzer sounds. That's the only way that you create an opportunity for the miracle to happen.

If you do what the average person does—what our built-in human nature tells us to do—you'll be just like every other average writer. Don't choose to be that average person! Remember: your thoughts and actions become a self-fulfilling prophecy.

Allow me to introduce you to your edge—the strategy that, when you use it, will skyrocket your goals and practically ensure every one of your ambitions is realized.

The Miracle Equation

Unwavering Faith + Extraordinary Effort = Miracles

It's easier than you think. The secret to maintaining unwavering faith is to recognize that it's a mindset and a strategy—it's not concrete. In fact, it's elusive. You can never make *every* sale. No athlete makes *every* shot. So, you have to program yourself to automatically have the unwavering faith to drive you to keep putting forth the extraordinary effort.

Remember, the key to putting this equation into practice, to maintaining unwavering faith in the midst of self-doubt, is the Miracle Mantra:

I will _____, no matter what. There is no other option.

For me recently, it was "My team will grow by 50 people this year, no matter what. There is no other option."

Once you set a goal, put that goal into the Miracle Mantra format. Yes, you're going to say your affirmations every morning (and maybe every evening, too). But all day, every day, you're going to repeat your Miracle Mantra to yourself. As you're driving or taking the train to the office, while you're on the treadmill, in the shower, in line at the grocery story, driving to pick up a prospect—in other words, *everywhere you go.*

Your Miracle Mantra will fortify your faith and be the self-talk you need to make just one more call or talk to one more person as they come through the door.

Bonus Lesson

Remember what I learned from my mentor, Dan Casetta: *The purpose of a goal isn't to hit the goal. The real purpose is to develop yourself into the type of person who can achieve your goals, regardless of whether you hit that particular one or not. It is who you become, by giving it everything you have until the last moment—regardless of your results—that matters most.*

You have to become the type of person who can achieve the goal. You won't always reach the goal, but you can become someone who maintains unwavering faith and puts forth extraordinary effort, regardless of your results. That's how you become the type of person you need to become to consistently achieve extraordinary goals.

And while reaching the goal almost doesn't matter (almost!), more often than not, you'll reach your goal. Do the elite athletes win every time? No. But they win most of the time. And you'll win most of the time, too.

At the end of the day, you can wake up earlier, do the Life S.A.V.E.R.S. with passion and excitement, get organized, focused, and intentional, and master every writing technique like a champ. And yet, if you don't combine unwavering faith with extraordinary effort, you won't reach the levels of writing success you seek.

The Miracle Equation gives you access to forces outside of anyone's understanding, using an energy that I might call God, the Universe, the Law of Attraction, or even good luck. I don't know how it works; I just know that it works.

You've read this far—you clearly want success more than almost anything. Commit to following through with every aspect of writing, including the Miracle Equation. You deserve it, and I want you to have it!

Putting It into Action:

1. Write out the Miracle Equation and put it where you will see it every day: Unwavering Faith + Extraordinary Effort = Miracles (UF + EE = M∞)

2. What's your number one goal for this year? What goal, if you were to accomplish it, would take your success to a whole new level?

3. Write your Miracle Mantra: I will _____ [insert your goals and daily actions, here], no matter what. There is no other option.

It is more about who you become in the process. You'll expand your self-confidence and, regardless of your results, the very next time you attempt to reach a goal, and every time after that, you'll be the type of person who gives it all they've got.

Closing Remarks

Congratulations! You have done what only a small percentage of people do: read an entire book. If you've come this far, that tells me something about you: you have a thirst for more. You want to become more, do more, contribute more, and earn more.

Right now, you have the unprecedented opportunity to infuse the Life S.A.V.E.R.S. into your daily life and business, upgrade your daily routine, and ultimately upgrade your life to a first class experience beyond your wildest dreams. Before you know it, you will be reaping the astronomical benefits of the habits that successful people use daily.

Five years from now, your life, business, relationships, and income will be a direct result of one thing: *who you've become*. It's up to you to wake up each day and dedicate time to becoming the best version of yourself. Seize this moment in time, define a vision for your future, and use what you've learned in this book to turn your vision into your reality.

Imagine a time just a few years from now when you come across the journal you started after completing this book. In it, you find the goals you wrote down for yourself—dreams you didn't even dare speak out loud at the time. And as you look around, you realize *your dreams now represent the life you are living*.

Right now, you stand at the foot of a mountain you can easily and effortlessly climb. All you need to do is continue waking up each day for your Miracle Morning and use the Life S.A.V.E.R.S. day after day, month after month, year after year, as you continue to take *yourself*, your *business*, and your *success* to levels beyond what you've ever experienced before.

Combine your Miracle Morning with a commitment to master your writing mastery skills, and use The Miracle Equation to create results that most people only dream of.

This book was written as an expression of what I know will work for you, to take every area of your life to the next level, faster than you may currently believe is possible. Miraculous performers weren't born that way—they have simply dedicated their lives to developing themselves and their skills to achieve everything they've ever wanted.

You can become one of them, I promise.

Taking Action: The 30-Day Miracle Morning Challenge

Now it is time to join the tens of thousands of people who have transformed their lives, incomes, and writing careers with *The Miracle Morning*. Join the community online at www.TMMBook. com and download the toolkit to get you started today.

A SPECIAL INVITATION FROM HAL

Fans and readers of *The Miracle Morning* make up an extraordinary community of like-minded individuals who wake up each day, dedicated to fulfilling the unlimited potential that is within all of us. As author of *The Miracle Morning*, it was my desire to create an online space where readers and fans could go to connect, get encouragement, share best practices, support one another, discuss the book, post videos, find an accountability partner, and even swap smoothie recipes and exercise routines.

I honestly had no idea that The Miracle Morning Community would become one of the most inspiring, engaged, and supportive online communities in the world, but it has. I'm blown away by the caliber of our 40,000+ members, which consists of people from all around the globe, and is growing daily.

Just go to **www.MyTMMCommunity.com** and request to join The Miracle Morning Community (on Facebook). Here you'll be able to connect with other individuals who are already practicing *The Miracle Morning*—many of whom have been doing it for years—to get additional support and accelerate your success.

I'll be moderating the community and checking in regularly. I look forward to seeing you there!

If you'd like to connect with me personally on social media, follow **@HalElrod** on Twitter and **Facebook.com/YoPalHal** on Facebook. Please feel free to send me a direct message, leave a comment, or ask me a question. I do my best to answer every single one, so let's connect soon!

ABOUT THE AUTHORS

HAL ELROD is the #1 best-selling author of what is now being widely regarded as "one of the most life-changing books ever written" (with over 1,331 five-star reviews on Amazon), *The Miracle Morning: The Not-So-Obvious Secret Guaranteed To Transform Your Life... (Before 8AM).* Hal died at age 20. Hit head-on by a drunk driver at 70 miles per hour, he broke 11 bones, was clinically dead for six minutes, spent six days in a coma, and was told he would never walk again. Defying the logic of doctors and the temptations to be a victim, Hal went on to not only walk but to run a 52 mile ultramarathon, become a hall of fame business achiever, an international keynote speaker, host of one of the top success podcasts on iTunes called *Achieve Your Goals with Hal Elrod*, and most importantly... he is grateful to be alive and living the life of his dreams with his wife, Ursula, and their two children, Sophie and Halsten. **For more information on Hal's speaking, writing, and coaching, please visit HalElrod.com.**

STEVE SCOTT is a top-rated self-published author who has written 40+ books, including one on *The Wall Street Journal's* Best Selling Books list. He currently runs two Internet businesses: **DevelopGoodHabits.com**, which teaches readers how to build one positive habit at a time, and **Authority. pub**, a blog and podcast that provides step-by-step information on the publishing process.

When he's not working, he enjoys traveling, hiking, running marathons, and spending time with his wonderful family.

HONORÉE CORDER is the best-selling author of more than a dozen books, including her runaway hit, *Vision to Reality: How Short Term Massive Action Equals Long Term Maximum Results*. Honorée's book has quickly become a must-read for every business professional who desires to go to the next level. For over 15 years, she has passionately served professionals and entrepreneurs as their coach, mentor, and strategic advisor. She empowers others to shed limiting beliefs, dream big, and go for what they truly want. Her mission is to inspire and motivate people to turn their vision and dreams into their real-life reality, sharing a leading-edge process she created for her executive coaching clients. Honorée's results-oriented philosophy and ground-breaking STMA 100-day Coaching Program has been embraced by people in a wide variety of industries and businesses, to rave reviews and exceptional results. **You can find out more about Honorée at HonoreeCorder.com.**

Made in the USA
Middletown, DE
11 June 2016